RUNNING OUTSIDE
of the BOX

How running 200 miles in a month changed my life
and how it could change yours

Running Outside of the Box

Published by The Conrad Press Ltd. in the United Kingdom 2022

Tel: +44(0)1227 472 874

www.theconradpress.com

info@theconradpress.com

ISBN 978-1-914913-70-9

Copyright © Ash Hurry, 2022

The moral right of Ash Hurry to be identified as author of this work has been asserted in accordance with the Copyright, Designs and Patents Act 1988.

All rights reserved.

Typesetting and Cover Design by: Charlotte Mouncey, www.bookstyle.co.uk
The Conrad Press logo was designed by Maria Priestley.

Printed and bound in Great Britain by Clays Ltd, Elcograf S.p.A.

RUNNING OUTSIDE
of the BOX

How running 200 miles in a month changed my life
and how it could change yours

Ash Hurry

Contents

Prologue	7
1. Getting going: How to make the first steps	20
2. Day one	22
3. My first half-marathon	31
4. Food glorious food	33
5. Breakfast of champions	35
6. Mistakes were made	39
7. Clothing	49
8. My shoes	51
9. Injuries	52
10. The second day	54
11. It's not over until it's over	62
12. Snooze	71
13. Breaking routine	81
14. Hobbies	91
15. Films	93
16. Football	98
17. Setbacks and struggles	105
18. The second day off	107
19. Four days to go	114
20. Triumph and reflection	124
21. Nearly there	126
22. Time	134
23. Victory	143
Epilogue	153
Running Log	155
Running Data	156
Acknowledgements	159

'Go fast enough to get there,
but slow enough to see.'

Jimmy Buffet

Prologue

I always thought 9/11 would be my generation's only insight into misery, dread and general shock due to a global event. Although 9/11 was an attack targeted on America, the whole world trembled that day. The world is trembling again now; trembling with confusion, trembling with uncertainty. The uncertainty is what's killing us.

We don't have a physical individual villain in this fight - it's not a terrorist with an agenda, nor is it a natural disaster like a super volcano, or even an 8.9 earthquake on the Richter scale. This is something worse. It's something physically affecting us, yet invisible. This invisible presence would then also trigger a raw psychological response within us and that in time would prove to be the real menace: ourselves.

I was twelve when it happened; I didn't really think much of it, but I knew something genuinely awful had happened. I was walking back from my secondary school in Basingstoke - I remember it was a pleasant hot day and I recall that it was also a lovely day in New York on that fateful Tuesday morning. The date now sends shivers down my spine and brings back feelings of sadness and confusion. In time the word, or acronym I should say, COVID-19, will in future decades evoke the same sort of feelings.

I made it back home and my parents were just watching the

news. Not emotional really, just in awe. My mum and dad are from Mauritius, so we've never really suffered the repercussions of the world wars in my family. Not to say there wasn't any struggle in their lives, but this was certainly a new perspective for them as much as it was for me, and the rest of the world. I was a little annoyed because my birthday was a few days later and it kind of stole my thunder. I was twelve, so forgive my selfishness.

As the years followed on, the anniversary of September 11th was always on the news accompanied with documentaries and experts talking about the collapse of the twin towers, Al-Qaeda, and the manhunt for Bin Laden. Conspiracy theories followed, films were made about it, people were playing devil's advocate - because a lot of thought was still being given to this event decades later, and it's strange to realise that I was alive when it happened, just like elderly people tell me they were there for the moon landing in 1969, or recount stories of World War II.

9/11 undoubtedly gave me a new perspective about life. This is where I started developing an understanding that the world can be brought down to its knees. We were vulnerable. We are vulnerable. It just takes one thing, and nothing really prepares you for it. You must just sit there, adapt to it and then move on. I've learnt to expect anything but never wait for it or look out for it, just live your life in spite of the madness of the world. Of course, as the years go on, the same documentaries are still on TV, and although the date is now in the past it has forever solidified itself in history, like the Chernobyl disaster, Vietnam or the Cuban Missile Crisis.

Nothing really prepares you for a pandemic. It just happens.

I mean I've seen films where outbreaks take place, and you watch the protagonists cope with it in the Hollywood way that they do, but that is the extent of my knowledge.

They said it started in Wuhan, China towards the end of 2019. I don't want to go into the specifics, and I could easily go into depth about it (especially because Google is just one click away from my word document) but at the time, that's all I heard. That's all anybody heard. It just kept popping up on television or on my phone. I should really turn off the news pop-up notifications on my phone but it's best to be informed (right?). Of course, later down the line, I Googled it and realise what this COVID-19 fuss was about.

I first heard about it around Christmas time in 2019. My girlfriend was round my house taking care of me, because I had recently dislocated my shoulder playing football. I played in goal and it was the first time ever I'd done something serious to my body. Just after I had turned thirty as well. The jokes were piling in from my friends, the usual banter that follows anything mildly negative that happens to you. Before I hurt my shoulder, I was running six days a week on the treadmill at my gym in Reading, usually clocking in about 3.8 miles. I always ran 12.5mph for thirty minutes. That was my routine. You become quite accustomed with numbers and stats when you really dig into a cardio routine, especially running. All that was put to a halt because of my stupid football injury.

So, I did what I always preached I wouldn't do. I started feeling sorry for myself, which consequently spun the spiral into eating junk food, and thus enjoyed the precautious comfort whilst I watched Christmas movies with Fran. Never broken a bone in my body and I've never had an operation, so I've been lucky in that aspect, but when the dislocated shoulder happened, I was just in a state of shock. I had no control over my body and that's what got to me.

It was an unusual feeling. I hated it. I did everything I could to heal as swiftly as I could. I did my shoulder exercises advised by my physio; I (eventually) ate the right stuff. I didn't aggravate my arm in anyway and I always kept the cast on. I was following the rules. Well, almost following the rules.

The day I took my cast off, which was two weeks after the preliminary injury, I went on the treadmill and ran. I did exactly the same speed and the same time. I figured my shoulder wouldn't be moving that much when I ran, I would keep it tucked in for most of it and be fine. (Well, fine in the sense that I could run again. Not fine in terms of how unfit I was!)

From the initial injury, it was one to two weeks of no physical activity whatsoever. Before dislocating my shoulder, aside from running, I was also playing football three times a week, I played pool twice a week at the Academy in Basingstoke, and every now and again I would play table tennis with some of my closest friends. So, those one to two weeks of pure isolation were a killer. I had no choice but to wait and heal.

The whole reason I run is because I want to be able to move around comfortably when I am older. I don't want to struggle. I hate having no control of my body. For the first time, I had a glimpse of that. This fuelled me even more, now that I had had a taste of it.

The other reason is because I like to eat. Let me rephrase

that: I like to eat rubbish. So, I don't feel so bad when I know I've done a good run. It's like a reward.

By the new year, I was fine and just doing my regular exercises. My left deltoid had dropped 1.2kg in mass because of it being in the sling for two weeks, so I continued doing shoulder exercises whenever I could.

Now that I had full control of my body again, I could start my routine again and get back into a sense of normal living.

2020. A new year. I was looking forward it. I think everyone was. 2019 wasn't that great – well, it was, but people were complaining about it and were just generally done with it by the time November had reached. Bring on the resolutions.

When a challenge arises, it's very hard to bat an eyelid to it. During lockdown people didn't have much to do. Some were not working because they were self-employed, others were furloughed and unfortunately, some lost their jobs. Those who were working, were working from home or in an isolated environment somewhere in an office. My girlfriend and I were both lucky. We were both working but both working from home. It was a strange but somewhat exciting time. I mean exciting in the most respectful and delicate way possible; people were dying, safety measures were being put in place but our lives, as we knew them, had changed and that sparked, for me, a certain excitement to it. It was something out of the norm and different. The nation had suddenly been given the gift of time and no one knew what to do with it.

It was around the end of March when lockdown was announced, and this meant simply: do not leave your homes. Don't go to work if you can work from home, and we were allowed only one-hour of exercise a day. It sounded like our prime minister was a prison warden giving us these strict rules and that is exactly how some of us felt: like prisoners. We couldn't socialise, we couldn't leave our homes unless it was for food, medicine and that one-hour-a-day for exercise. Now being the typical Brits that we are, people were provoked not to follow rules but were later shown just how stupid that was.

The one-hour rule where we could exercise had inspired everyone to be runners and fitness freaks. It wasn't a bad thing, just slightly unusual. People were taking advantage of the hour they had outside to finally start running, which made no sense to me. I had always promoted the notion of going for runs, and I always said there is literally no excuse in the world that can stop you from running, short of lack of limbs. You normally go to work and then you come home. People were now working from their homes and then going running. I mean what is the difference, between pre-lockdown and now? It's amazing what things can push or trigger you.

It started to pick up like any trend does on social media. Run five, nominate five - where you would run five kilometres and then nominate five other people to do the run, whilst raising funds for charity. I mean I talk about this in a negative fashion, but people were getting fitter and donating to charity. Who cares if it was a trend? That fact that it was a trend was the sole reason why people decided to do it. The real reason behind my negativity is that it was spring. And spring means hay fever. If you've ever had hay fever, it's one of the worst things to endure. Okay, I'm being dramatic, there are worse things I'm sure - but hay fever isn't nice. The itchy eyes, the sore throat, the runny nose and, in my case, my asthma being triggered.

I was born with asthma and I've never really had the major symptoms for long. Never carried an inhaler and I've never had an attack. But some years, during the spring season, more specifically when the tree pollen is high, it will trigger my asthma and then I normally carry an inhaler as I'm at risk of having an attack. This year it was close, because I was so adamant to keep on running and follow these trends people were doing, I pushed myself a little harder than I should have.

We were mid-April, and the fitness trends were off the charts. People were doing live videos of their workouts and documenting the runs they just did. The tables had turned. I was so used to going running in the early hours of the morning, sticking it on social media long before anyone else was up, and then going to work. But now, because of my hay fever, I couldn't, and everyone else that wasn't running before was now smashing it. What made matters worse was that I was told the symptoms for hay fever are worryingly like those of COVID-19. It was a momentary scare where your mind entertains your worse fear but fortunately, I just had hay fever. Lucky me.

There was a moment where people were controversially bumping up their 5k run scores on whatever platform that had used to advertise them. It was then I found out people were not doing it for the right reasons. It's just a matter of perception. It's a matter of *I'm doing it too*. Now the competitive side to me was always glancing twice at the times, because it's in my nature to do so.

I ran the 5k once in 19.53 but that was some time ago. Anything below 24.30, I would be happy with. I should really say it doesn't matter about the time; but in my head it does. After not running with any real success or rhythm for the best part of two months because my gym in Reading had closed due to COVID, which was then followed in astounding timely fashion by my hay fever, and now with everyone broadcasting their Olympic-worthy times on social media, I had to get involved.

My friend, Ryan, went out there and did it in twenty-nine minutes. He's a very good runner and that is a very good time. One child in the picture and another on the way, he still found the time to run. So, I said to myself, *screw this, let's go*. I didn't care about the asthma; I just stuck my trainers on and went outside without thinking twice about it.

It was a remarkable clusterfuck. I lasted 1.5k with the hope to make myself feel better and beat my friend's time. This was when I had, or almost had, my first asthma attack. I didn't tell anyone. I simply walked home huffing and puffing very violently until I got my inhaler and just did nothing for an hour. My girlfriend didn't even notice, and I made sure she didn't. She would have brought the walls down every time I went out for a run.

Towards mid-April I went out again and went a little further but once again I fell short and once again, almost had another attack. This was ridiculous. The second run was triggered because I was nominated to run 5k and I couldn't turn down a friendly old challenge. I mean I was running six kilometres in thirty minutes pre-COVID so those two runs were a real kick in the teeth. I had fallen dramatically. I realised I had to wait until my hay fever had passed and fortunately, it did towards the end of April.

One day, I gathered I wasn't breathing heavily anymore when I took a walk to the shop, which mirrors part of my running route. I tested the waters. I jogged for thirty minutes as slow as possible and I felt great. By the time May had come I had completed three to four runs back-to-back, but very sluggishly. I think I ran 3.4 miles in thirty minutes. The hay fever was gone, and it was time to somehow shed all this weight I had put on. The momentum was there.

There were memes going on about people putting on weight during isolation. And it was true; I had, and people had too. During isolation when I was waiting for my hay fever to pass, I ordered a racket and played tennis, I read three books, I watched films, I was learning bits of Italian, I learned a few new things to cook, so it was time well spent; but I was also racking up the weight too. I did some weightlifting at home with the mediocre dumbbells that I have, but I never really enjoyed weightlifting. In my head if you sweat, then it's a workout and I believe you can do that in running, very effortlessly. It's just you and your mind and it's quite the journey. When you get to a certain point when running, you actually start to enjoy it. That's where I wanted to go. That is where I wanted to be.

May 1st hit, and the weather was baking. I think that May ended up being the hottest spring on record. Of course, no one was there to enjoy it in a social manner. Thanks, COVID.

I had noticed these challenges kept appearing on social media. Have you noticed that advertisements on social media, or on your phone, are strangely accurate to what you were previously talking about in person with someone? I was talking about getting my teeth straightened and suddenly there were advertisements on dentures and the best places to go on my phone. I'm not even going to think about it, because I probably already know the answer if I went looking for it.

Anyways, over the weekend I was dusting off my medals and I counted them and realised right there and then, that I wanted to set myself a goal, to have fifty medals before I'm fifty. Kind of an asshole thing I know, but it was a goal. It was a challenge. It was right there, that this mind set of having a goal, got the wheels turning in my head.

I have twelve for running at the moment. Have some trophies for other things though like football and tennis, but I'm not counting them. So, I thought: let's gain my fitness back and do a lot more events by having this incentive I have created for myself. My social media was covered with challenges, all these advertisements for running, doing virtual runs and getting a medal for it and this was all because of the running events, the marathons and half-marathons now being cancelled due to COVID. Run fifty miles in May and whatnot. Granted I Googled events on my phone, so I wasn't as surprised that advertisements were coming up.

One night when Fran and I were watching a film, I checked my phone and my friend posted a picture of a medal on Instagram of doing hundred miles in April. I used to work with her a long time ago, so I messaged her, and we got talking about it. After fifteen minutes of talking to her, I signed up for the May running challenge, even though it was four days into May. That's right, Star Wars Day.

I paid around thirteen pound to take part. At the end I

would get a medal with the number miles I ran engraved on it. The miles varied from twenty to two-hundred. I didn't even think about the two-hundred miles - I would just match my friend who had already completed a hundred miles in April. I didn't bat an eyelid. I signed up and on May 4th I ran 3.7 miles, which would end up being my usual route. Things work better when you have a goal, when you have a purpose.

By May 30th I completed the hundred miles with my girlfriend; she even ran with me on ten of the twenty-six runs I did. When I went running on May 29th, I realised I had developed a rhythm, I couldn't stop, and instinctively I was going to do another hundred miles in June. Without a moment's hesitation and for some ungodly reason, I signed up for June for two-hundred miles on my day off on the 31st May. I told everyone about it. I advertised it; I even had my friend talk me into doing it for charity, which was a great idea. And he even donated twenty-five quid the second I had the donations page up and running. I had raised sixty percent of my target before my first run. There was no backing out.

So, the night before June 1st, I did the maths. I had to run 6.7 miles every day without a rest. Fuck June for having thirty days. The most I ran in May was five miles. When I did the maths again in my head, I immediately regretted what I had got myself into, but something had been sparked in me now, and it wasn't going to stop. I had energy and a determination to test my limits now.

It was the evening before June. I went for a walk and I scouted the path I was going to run for seven miles. *Jesus, am I really going to run seven miles every day?* Fuck me. I walked all the way to Palmer Park, which was less than a mile away from my flat. Palmer Park is about seventy-one acres and has a path that runs around the outside of it. It was perfect for my challenge. It's about a mile for a full lap, give or take. That's five laps and then run back on London Road and back to the flat. That's around seven miles. I knew this was what I would be doing for the next thirty days. Why the hell did I agree to this though? How did I manage to instinctively do this?

It's good to have doubt because it means what you're about to do is going to be challenging and so worth doing, and I knew in my heart I was going to do this. I had to, but I hadn't figured out why yet.

This pandemic has done some funny things to us. It cancelled weddings, restaurants weren't open anymore, we couldn't even socialise outside, film productions stopped. The world was frozen, but we were still moving. And by god, I needed to make sure I was still moving.

When 9/11 happened, all I thought about was my birthday being ruined, all I thought about was why this was such an important event; why this event is remembered, why 9/11 is not just a date anymore. Then it came to me. We are only here for moments. Time just doesn't hang around. When 9/11 happened, my memory was of everyone mourning, in sadness and in shock. It really was. But what I was too young to see were the firefighters there twenty-four hours a day, the army leading the hunt for Bin Laden, the construction workers cleaning up New York, the air traffic controllers performing magic during the height of emotion, and the people who built Ground Zero.

You see, when something bad happens the world stops for a second but time carries on. How long you stop depends entirely on you. It's about adapting to any given situation, learning how to do that.

I'm lucky, I realised, with my dislocated arm and then again with COVID-19. People decided to stop, people froze. But we clapped our hands on Thursdays every week, we showed gratitude and people were raising money for charities. I wanted to be a really small part of it. I don't care about my birthday being ruined or any birthdays, I shouldn't care about restaurants not being open. I care that everyone is still moving. Some will have to move through obstacles, some bigger than others - but this is also an opportunity to use time when it's given to you. I had no doubt I was going to do this challenge but at the same time nothing prepared me for how hard it was going to be.

1) Challenges are about discovery, not ego.

2) The world has been brought down to its knees and something may bring it down again. Just make sure you're still moving, and the world will keep on spinning.

3) Doubt is good because it means what you're doing is worth it.

1
Getting going:
How to make the first steps

The very first form of transport was walking - and then someone decided to jump on an animal, a donkey, an elephant, or a horse, and from there, things just progressed. Someone invented the wheel; someone else made an engine; and here we are today. The sky was apparently the limit at one point - an outdated expression now that there's a footprint on the moon. We reached the heights of something spectacular, and the imagery is the flag, and that footprint. We went back to basics. We walked on the moon. One foot in front of the other and the pace on getting there depends entirely on you. So simple, so effective, so efficient. Why walk anywhere? Because we can, we are designed to.

I never really thought about running and what it would do to me. There's no skill in it, virtually everyone can do - but many don't, maybe because of the simplicity of it. All you need is you and your shoes. When starting out, you can overload your mind with the *right* way of doing it; but things can just be simple. It's what's best for you. You don't really need to worry about shoes, the outfit you wear right away - that comes later. If you are just starting out, get a connection with the open road and what your body is saying to you. Doctors' number one tip is always listen to your body.

I went out in my school shoes and jeans for my first ever run that wasn't a cross country PE lesson, just to see how far I could go. I ran for five minutes. And in that five minutes, I learnt that my body didn't like the jeans I was wearing, and it didn't like me running, mainly because I was unfit. So, the next day I ran six minutes, and I wore shorts this time. As you keep progressing, your common sense will tell you what's best for you. Don't worry about anything. Just run. And the rest will fall into place. You want to run in a fancy dress outfit, you go right ahead; you want to break some personal best records, then that's where your initiative comes in and that's where you will see what the best trainers or outfits are for you. Remember, it's just one small step. That's how everything begins and it's the hardest part. Take the first step and watch what happens. The sky's the limit.

2
Day one

This wasn't going to be easy. I was glad it wasn't because otherwise anyone could do it. It must be hard for it to be worth it. It's a contradiction of the mind - but that's how it works.

I lost some weight in May from running but only a little, since I was also consuming a lot of food. And it wasn't even healthy either. I'm guilty of eating appallingly. The reason I'm talking about weight is, in my head, the lighter I am, the easier it will be to run. That's the logic, right? I figured all that running in May should have got me a little lighter, but with burning that much energy, you must also consume a lot as well.

Two-hundred miles, however, is another level. I need to keep my energy up for this. It's not about losing weight. It's about completing the two-hundred miles. At any cost, even if I must fill up on carbs. 6.7 miles a day, just thinking about it was killing me inside.

I remember going to Mauritius for a month every summer and I would run every day there for two hours. So, I knew I could do it and my body has done it before - but Jesus, how long ago was that?

I also remember in 2015 I ran consecutively for a hundred and ninety-six days on the treadmill. Running thirty minutes every day. It became a habit because after day fifty, which was my initial target, I had to keep doing it, and I just kept going.

I was still quite heavy, carrying a lot of fat on my sides, but I guessed that was going to serve as energy. Around late mid-May, closer to the end of May, I ordered some new Nike running shoes because my Asics were destroyed. I figured if I'm going to get through to June, I need things to look forward to.

These little things that were in my mind, were like mental landmarks for me to keep going. I would do the same thing when running, picking visual landmarks. I would need to get past this tree, or this lamppost and it served as another thing to overcome the pain in my body when I ran. Having things to look forward to is very important. It gives you purpose, no matter how small it may be. With this fucking virus, there were a lot of things to look forward to after lockdown. Eating in restaurants again, live sports recommencing and going back to the cinema but sometimes you must create your own targets, your own little goals.

So, my shoes, my medals and of course my football were mine.

I had decided, after talking to a few people, I would of course need a rest day. I knew I needed one, but I've always been very stubborn with rest days because it breaks routine, as you must know now from me running a hundred and ninety-six days straight, but I needed to be sensible here. I decided to run seven miles every day which meant I was building up 0.3 miles of credit, because all I had to run to meet the two-hundred miles in thirty days, was doing 6.7 miles a day. I figured if I did seven miles a day, I would have only one rest day the entire month and one of my runs would be cut down to 5.2 miles instead of seven. That was the plan. Although, things hardly ever go to plan, do they?

Many would be against it, but this was the schedule I chose to do.

I also chose to wake up at six am and run it then, because it would be nice and cool and not scorching hot. I learnt the hard way when I didn't wake up one morning in May and ran when I got back from work in the evening. It was boiling. Twenty-six degrees I think, and the park was packed, with children and cyclists everywhere. So, I figured doing seven miles in twenty-six degrees in Palmer Park, packed to the brim, wouldn't be such a great idea.

In the morning it's quiet, there's no children running around in the park, no cyclist, there's hardly any other runners and also the traffic, there will be none, which means no fumes or exhaust. However, I would only be spending about fifteen percent of my run near cars, the rest would be in the park where it's pure oxygen from the trees. I scouted the route, and this was the best route for me.

It was the day of, and I was up bright and early. 6.10am and it was a nice a sunny day. Perfect running conditions, sunny but still with that morning chill. I wore my Captain America top to feel special. I decided in May that I would be recording my runs via *Relieve;* this app which gives you a 3D breakdown of your run, which I thought was pretty cool. I needed an app to prove that I had done the hundred miles in May. On the last day of the month, the Virtual run team would ask proof of your runs.

The night before, it felt like the next morning was the first day of school, butterflies in my stomach kind of feeling. The reason for this was simply because I wasn't actually sure I could do this, however I knew I had to somehow, no matter what. The hundred miles in May I knew deep down, I could do so I never really doubted myself, but this was something else entirely. I acted like this was my prison time and each run were going to bring me closer to my release day.

The best advice I got was from Richard. We met back when I was going to the gym in Basingstoke. He was a trainer there. He was also always giving me the thumbs up when he saw me running during those one hundred and ninety-six days on the treadmill, as he was in most days. And with that, we got talking about running and he became a good friend. He was a seasoned runner who had done over ninety marathons and he even made me a little video at my request for some tips on resting and how he would approach it. I asked for this a couple of days prior when I was advertising my JustGiving page.

I had my phone ready, my wireless headphones on, connected via Bluetooth and my flat keys. I chose *Rope* for my first run. Alfred Hitchcock, the dialogue in his films always brings me in. I didn't need to see it; I knew the movie quite well. And that was the point of me choosing it.

Now, Richard told me one important thing: when running, never worry about the time, just finish the run. Back when people were doing the run five nominate five, all I was looking at was the time, who I was or wasn't better than. This mindset had to leave my head. I was battling myself. We usually are in life.

In my head, I knew running seven miles below an hour was

quite good, but there was no way I could do that every day for a month. *Well, why not,* a little voice in my head said. *Why can't I do that?* There were too many things going on in my head that didn't need to be there but of course, that's another battle. I just had to run. One foot in front of the other. I couldn't walk any of it; it was jog, sprint or run. Never a walk.

I posted a picture on my social feed. It was 6.11 in the morning. It read, *It begins* I scouted the route the day before but here I am right now, jogging it. It had begun.

My pace was good and steady. It's about 0.6 miles from my flat until I reach the back entrance to Palmer Park. Those 0.6 Miles is running alongside London Road, past Cemetery junction and down the A329 on Wokingham Road until I hit the park. The first day is always the hardest because you're not in routine yet, you're settling in.

When running past Tesco's at 6.20ish in the morning, there was a courier bringing fresh bread in. Smelt amazing. I guess that's something I can add to my mental map in my head. When approaching the park, it was good, no vehicles, no fumes and it wasn't raining. I hoped it wouldn't rain for the next month, at least not in the mornings.

Palmer Park is covered with tall trees along the pathways and I would be running underneath them, providing shelter from any precipitation, so that is always good - although it was June, it was summer, I didn't think it was going to be raining anytime soon, especially after having the hottest May on record. But it was one of the reasons why I chose this route. A lot of people were telling me to mix my route up during this challenge. It's always good listening to advice, gives you a different perspective - however, the decision is always down to you. And nine times out of ten, you usually go with your own decision.

After Lap one, I was fine. I was doing okay, all that was in my head, however, was my own thoughts, not the voice of Jimmy Stewart.

Lap two came around slowly and it was starting to hurt. I wanted to stop. That's all I wanted to do. I wasn't exactly thin, and my trainers had taken a beating through May so maybe that was probably what it was. The truth is, all the runs I was doing only involved two, maybe three laps max around the park. It was the realisation that I wasn't even halfway done, and that gave me a sucker punch to the gut. I can't stop running now. Thing is, you're going to entertain every doubt in your head, especially when you run. People run to clear their heads and what that means is that they are going through a physical pain with their body so your mind will either try to make you stop, or distract you with whatever main thoughts you have, and they're usually things that you're worried about, or scare you. Well, I was getting all of that rubbish and it was all to do with this run, and that's very common. You must distract yourself. You must dig in and really fight your way into your routine.

I put Hitchcock on for a reason, so let's listen to it. I'm running in a park with hardly anyone here, so don't complain; let's just get this done. Before I knew it, I was on lap three. I knew at some point, I needed to check my app to see how far I had run, but I didn't yet.

By lap five, I realised that this was the furthest I had run in a while and my legs were getting tired. All I cared about right then, was just finishing that run, not worrying about anything else. Another thing that was looming over my head was that the second I'd finish, I would still have the whole day ahead of me and then back at it tomorrow. This couldn't be easy and I'm glad it wasn't. I wanted to do this and to be able to say I've done it and know it was hard. This mind set boosted me for the rest of the run. It was five laps.

The south exit of Palmer Park on the 5th lap brought me to 6.1 miles so I left the park and was on London Road, which is on the other side of the park from where I entered. It's a little longer; it goes straight past Cemetery Junction and down London Road to my flat. I was jogging along paths with people walking and shops opening and suddenly I had more to look at. I had to time my pace because I had to cross London Road as the path runs out and if I stopped, I knew it would be game over for me. Remember, I can't walk, and I can't stop. Not yet anyways.

I ran past Cemetery Junction; I could see the Tesco's on the other side of the road. It seemed like a lifetime ago I ran past the smell of fresh bread. From there, it was a straight road down from London Road to the flat. I checked the Relive app. 6.5 miles. 'Well, this is shit,' I thought. I was almost at the flat and I still had half a mile to go. I predicted I would have to run past my flat and keep going until I hit 6.9 and then turn around and that's exactly what I did, a bit demoralising running past the flat but I did it. I had to. This was expected from the day before, when I scouted the route.

In my head I knew all I really needed to do was 6.7 miles, but I needed a day off and that extra 0.3 miles every day would eventually add up to one. My phone was out, and it was displaying my time and mileage. I was counting down the metres and finally, the app read seven miles. I stopped running but I kept moving, always moving. I was walking very slowly. My legs were jelly. Part of me had forgotten all about the next twenty-nine days. Today was a victory and I felt great. Seven miles were in the bag. One-hundred and ninety-three to go. It took me an hour and three minutes to do it. Almost four minutes actually.

This would be my routine. This would be what I would be doing every morning.

I got back from work that day - yes, I had work. I felt great knowing I had just done seven miles, but as the day drew to a close the glum realisation was I would have to do this over and over again. But it's about getting into that mind set.

Twenty-nine days were ahead of me, I needed small things, I needed reasons to look forward to something, to get out of my bed and to do that run. I had my shoes coming now, they were cool - free runs, black and, of course, Nike. Only a few days to wait for them now.

1) The first day is the most important and the hardest. Once you get through that, you have created awareness on what is to come. The key is to keep creating awareness. The more consistent you are, the more aware you become of what you are doing and with that, comes progress.

2) Give yourself things to look forward, no matter how small. You have to stay grounded at all times and remind yourself of everyday things to help you fuel your challenge.

3) Planning is always good but always expect things to deviate from the original plan. Expecting it makes you more adaptable to any situation, especially when it's to do with your own thought out plans.

3

My first half-marathon

My first half marathon was in 2014 in Wokingham. My friend Ryan got us to do it and I didn't take it seriously at all. In my head, I thought I could do it - and I wasn't wrong, but the journey was both an eye opener, and extremely painful. I had a Domino's Pizza the day before and my shoes were not even running shoes. I just wasn't prepared for it at all, I hadn't run more than five miles before that day - I didn't train for it at all. I think I mainly did it because Ryan said he could do it, and so in my head, I could do it. I was stupidly competitive back then. Ryan was ten times fitter than I was at that point. He carried me during that run, mentally speaking.

First mile went well, and I was getting all cocky; I decided to increase my speed. However shortly after, it was a disaster. It was pretty much all uphill, and no, not literally, although it could have fooled me - the amount of pain I was going through was absurd. At running events, they have these placards that tell you what mile you're at when you run past them, so naturally in a half marathon there are thirteen placards.

It wasn't until we got to the tenth placard that I had my first experience of the term 'second wind' and it was only triggered by one thing: a double-digit number.

The agony in running ten miles whilst seeing a placard reading one then two then three, every single mile, was both painful and just not beneficial whatsoever. I was completely done, mentally, by mile five, and I knew it was thirteen miles so, when ten popped around the corner it just gave me a boost and from that, it's still an experience I'll never forget.

After that ten-mile point in Wokingham however, I stopped around mile eleven. So that second wind didn't last long, but I'll never forget that feeling of that boost to go another level. I didn't control it, I got overexcited with this boost of adrenaline and that day, was the first and only time I stopped during a long-distance race. Ryan really had to push me, talks of Burger King kept me from stopping completely, and we finally finished the Wokingham Half-Marathon in two hours and twenty-three minutes, or something along those lines. For the next two weeks, I was hobbling around right like I had just been shot in the leg.

Today, when I woke up, I thought of those memories in Wokingham. Who would have thought, that would have been the start of many runs to come? I was never really into running before that but it's amazing how one experience can change everything.

4

Food glorious food

Someone somewhere will tell you at some point to eat something that you don't like. That's fine but that famous saying is true: you are what you eat. You eat junk, you're going to feel like junk. You drink water instead of fizzy drinks, you're going to feel better.

I'm not here to judge - who am I to judge anyway? I'm not exactly the fitness guru myself. All I will say is this, and this is this the mindset that got me through running: the physical fight is the run; your mental fight is your diet, because you have to have the will power not to consume rubbish. I ate a Domino's pizza the day before my first half-marathon. Yes, carbs are good - but not those carbs! I paid for it; I struggled and laboured, and I learnt a lesson that day. The physical run is only half the battle, maybe not even that. Keep it light, keep it sensible and above else don't be greedy.

My general rule for training is very simple: you know what's bad and you know what's good. Be smart about that. The only thing you should drink is water. It's so important to stay hydrated. Your body is around sixty percent water and you're going to sweat when you run - you want to sweat! I aim to drink two litres a day. It's all about intuition. We know chocolate is bad and fruit is good. They both will give you the sugar that will need to do the job. Don't go to a hotel breakfast buffet before a run - you know this! Keep it light. Two crumpets with a dash of jam. Porridge. Oatmeal. A cup of coffee, and that is the only time when you will be drinking something other than water. Try not to eat after eight pm. Truth is, you can make your own rules, your own system, whatever works for you - but you have to be clever about it.

People follow rules and rules are too strict sometimes. You have to be balanced in your thinking. Light snacks before running and guess what: you're going to feel light during the run. I am not going to give you a list of what to eat and what not to eat - experience will surely tell you what your body doesn't like and what your body can make do with.

My lesson to you is simply: be smart about it.

5
Breakfast of champions

After half hour of being awake in bed, Fran had gotten up and I soon followed. She made coffee and breakfast whilst I was setting the table and putting on some background sound on the TV. Not the news. Something like *Planet Earth*. We had cinnamon swirls that Fran baked the day prior. Fran was also making pancakes, something she learnt during lockdown and she's got the technique down pretty well. I had two of those straight after the cinnamon swirls. She was secretly treating me because we sort of had a day off together - meaning I was off, and she was working from home, but she takes regular breaks snuggling with me in bed or just hanging out in front of the TV. The fact is we were taking advantage of being together. It was nice.

I had two pancakes and two swirls and a big cup of coffee. The second I finished it though, I looked at my phone to check the time and I knew, in exactly two hours I would go for my run. Give time for the food to sink in and for the energy to be used for those seven miles. That was always the way I did that if I had breakfast before the run.

Most days I ran on an empty stomach resorting to the fat in my love handles has energy. 11.30 came around, which was the two-hour mark.

I also realised this week was going to be hot. I think with the rain we had last week, I will know which I will hate the most: running in the scorching heat or running in the pouring rain.

I deliberately decided to run near midday when the sun was at its highest because I wanted my body to get use to the heat. Just get a feel of it. Not exactly the fourteen-day acclimatisation they do in Morocco or California, but it's what I got available to me in the time given.

I had finished reading *The Fear Bubble* and Anthony Middleton was explaining that when he was at Base Camp at Everest, they would do these rotations where they would go to camp one and then return back to Base Camp, then they would stay there and then go back to camp one, stay there for a day, go to camp two, which was a big climb and after even going to camp three, they would then descend all the way back to Base Camp and then do it again before summiting.

There was four camps before the final push to the summit. Camp four is better known as the 'The Death Zone', eight-thousand feet above sea level, less than forty percent oxygen in the air. You can only stay there a maximum of three days otherwise, that's game over.

They would keep doing this for weeks just so their body would adapt to the thin air and it would acclimatize their body. I mean I wasn't worried about altitude, but I was tackling my own Everest.

I knew running in the heat would prepare my body for the tough weeks ahead. In my head I still hadn't decided if I was going to split my runs or do them in the morning.

11.30 and it was hot. Not mad hot, but you know hot

enough to make you sweat if you were to jump up and down for a couple of minutes. Weather would invite a lot of runners and most people are furloughed at the moment so most likely that Palmer Park will be full.

I only ran 1.5 mile and I felt terrible. My stomach felt hollow. I felt just dead. This was something new, something that I thought hurt more than usual but that's always the case when you're in the moment.

How was I meant to run around Palmer Park like this? Benefit of going through hell is you can compare it to something you would normally bitch about. I just need to grind through.

I carried on and realised that this happened to me already on a few of the other runs. Your body is trying to tell you to stop, it's getting to a point now where I'm really stretching what my body can do. It wasn't until mile three or four that this second wind had kicked in. I mentally told myself I would be okay after lap three and I was.

Some people give up too early but sticking things out always benefits you, because your chances go up. Yes, playing the lottery is probably never going to happen in your lifetime, even if you played once a week. But you're sticking it out and just by doing that, you're going to have more chances of winning, unlikely, virtually impossible but mathematically speaking, your probability is higher.

Another good example is Andy Murray. I love my tennis and I consider it one of the hardest sports to play, hence why I respect tennis players. The whole sport is based on respect, between one player and another, like boxing. But with tennis, the stamina you need to be able to last five sets is extraordinary.

Hand eye coordinating, fitness, planning your next shot, your footwork, where your opponent is going to hit the serve.

Now with Andy Murray, when someone like Djokovic or Nadal and Federer hit a deep shot, a shot that some, in fact most wouldn't even attempt to hit back because it was a winning shot by the opponent, Andy Murray would hit the ball back from all the way back on the base line, out of position, his back turned, his legs sliding in god knows what position, his opponent probably at the net ready to slam it.

And nine times out of ten, he just made his opponent play one more shot but the more and more he kept making those returns, the more he kept making his opponents play one more shot, the higher the probability of them making an unforced error is or a higher probability for him to stay in the game.

You see giving up is a done deal, you're out, but if you grind your way through and just stick with it, the chance, the possibility of succeeding, of winning, is always going to be there. By that third mile, I held on long enough to start feeling my body ease into this run. It's like life, you need to stick at things, no matter how laborious things get.

-

You have to sometimes experience the full consequences of your error to learn from it. When running you have to be sensible when it comes to eating, especially if you're training for a long-distance run. You may be able to get away with it on a five-kilometre run but still don't be fooled when it comes to diet. It's a pain you don't want when you run. Stay away from heavy fast food. Try and eat six small meals. Stick to the light food - not two bloody cinnamon swirls and pancakes! I wasn't being smart.

6

Mistakes were made

Sometimes mistakes happen more than once; and sometimes one time isn't enough to learn from it. That's life really.

My stomach was still full from yesterday's meal. We had a huge katsu curry that Fran made, and she didn't eat some of hers, so I stepped in and ate hers too. I don't know why she didn't finish her meal, when we usually go to Wagamama, there is usually nothing left, and this is after starters too.

Wagamama - just one of many things I'm missing during this lockdown. You could still order through Deliveroo or UberEATS, but it just wasn't the same. People don't go to restaurants for the food, they go for the atmosphere, they go to relax, and food happens to be part of this experience.

Restaurants are all about your surroundings, the service, and the interactions. It's just being able to take a break from cooking, a break from your familiar surroundings, to dress up and go somewhere, and there's something about being served that puts a smile on your face.

I wouldn't order it unless I was gagging for it, it's a package deal for me. I have to eat Wagamama's at the restaurant.

McDonalds or Burger King on the other hand, is another story. You're there for mainly the food, a cheap eat, though when you were a kid, it was for those fun houses they had. Enticed you right in at a young age, didn't they? Thinking about it, I don't think I've had a McDonald at all this year. New personal challenge maybe?

Piling up on the carbs is always good, particularly when you're running seven miles every day. You'd figured I would have digested it by now but nope, still kicking around, still feeling bloated.

I was up at six on the dot just like yesterday. I deliberately ignored the windows and just went straight to the toilet. The toilet was acting as my place of purgatory. I was here after the run, before the run. I was in there reading the news, ranting about the news, sobbing over the weather amongst other distractions from outside the bathroom door.

Looking through my phone while I sat there fuming, I knew all I was doing, was just procrastinating. Saying that though, even after you're finished on the toilet, you always tend to just stay there for a while because you know, no one will disturb you. It's a peaceful place.

I looked at my weather app and saw to my instantaneous disappointment that it was in fact, raining. Didn't even need to check outside, could hear it the second I woke up. It was possibly the damn rain that's been waking me up so sharply these past couple of days.

After about ten minutes, I was getting irritated. Nothing was coming out of me and yet here I'm sat on the toilet bloated and needing to go. I haven't got time for this right now; I need to get going. I can't get too comfortable. Remember, nothing is attained through a comfort zone.

I did my press ups in the confidence that I would trigger myself, but to my displeasure and irritation, nothing gave way. It was already half six. I wasn't methodical today at all - so much for doing things differently. The sound of the rain was a sucker punch to the gut especially after doing it yesterday. I just thought, or assumed, the worst was over. Saying that, a sucker punch to the gut would positively help me go to the toilet right now.

I think in my mind, I wasn't presuming for it to happen again. It's a dangerous thing, expectations.

In the desperation of getting ready, I forgot my shoes were outside the flat from the previous day. I opened the door and thankfully saw they were still there; they haven't been stolen. They were still wet though, and they were about to be even wetter. My shorts had dried, and I put on a new top. You should have seen my top yesterday, mixture of sweat and rain and that fucking puddle that was looming conveniently around the exit of the park.

Just avoid getting taken out by a puddle was the key mental note for this run, as invigorating as it was it did nothing for me now. As I slid my foot in my shoe, I could feel the dampness and just like that, my socks were already wet. This was the first time my eyes were over half open. The dampness of my sock's contact with my shoes and now feet just sent an electric shock throughout my body, which in effect, started putting my mind in gear.

Without even peeking outside, with my head down, I walked towards the door, and I stepped outside. I was like a grumpy school child. Well, it was raining but it wasn't as bad as yesterday. It was a substantial drizzle - nonetheless, still annoying.

Before I even got to Cemetery Junction, which was 0.5 miles away from my flat, I was not feeling great. I felt cold. I was shattered and I was dragging my legs. And worst of all, I was still bloated.

I realised I hadn't properly woken myself up in the morning. I only semi woke up when I put my shoes on in the communal area.

I didn't take the two minutes to wake up. I was just faffing around the place. I did the essentials, had some water, did my press ups but didn't take a minute to get prepared. I mean, I was on the toilet chilling, but I was half asleep whilst sat there and just agonizing about the weather.

By mile two, I really needed to go for a shit. And usually, if you fart during a run, that's a good sign, releasing some air and that's always good, because it makes you a little lighter and hopefully that heaviness you're carrying around, goes away.

However, when you think you need to fart and you try to and nothing, you're in a spot of bother. Now I remember a time when I went on the treadmill and I would always run thirty minutes and fifteen seconds religiously and when the gym opens again, I'm sure I'll return to that. So, this one time I hopped on the treadmill and I was only running for two minutes, if that, and it hit me, I really needed to go to the toilet.

One of the very few benefits about running outside is that you can let one rip whenever you want, especially in the morning when it's raining and there's no one there. Shitting yourself is another matter. By mile three, I was scanning Palmer Park for subtle places to go where no one would see me. However, that means I would have to stop and then I would totally have to void the three miles I had already done. Well, I wouldn't but it would really annoy me to a level. I'd rather just shit myself and carry on running. Eskimo dogs, the ones that pull the sled in the Nordic countries are known to run and shit at the same time. Now, that's multitasking for you.

Anyways the point I was making on the treadmill was, on minute two, I knew I had to go and it kept trying to come out and there were periods where it would come and go. With just focusing on random rubbish and just trying not to think about it, I managed to finish the run without shitting myself. The second I finish however, I didn't do my usual cool down, I subtly power walked upstairs and went to the toilet. What a feeling. Holding a shit for the longest time and then finally going is just one of those moments everyone I'm sure has experienced.

But I knew the time scale, I knew my surroundings, I knew exactly when I was going to finish. I knew in twenty-eight minutes I would be done, which in a way makes it worse because, when I got to twenty-nine minutes with one minute left, my body knew I was close, so I needed to go more and when I finished, I did everything in double speed.

Why didn't I just jump up and down when I was at home, instead of just waiting to go toilet or just wake up earlier, or not had Fran's portion last night.

All these *What if* moments started overflowing into my head. What's done is done but regardless, you can't help but accommodate those thoughts.

We had prunes in the house; I could have eaten them maybe. Prunes have a source of laxative in them, as does most fruits but I don't eat fruit. I haven't eaten a piece of fruit since I was three years old. My body just rejects it. Bananas are the worst. I despise them. The thought of one makes me want to puke. I hate everything about them, the smell, and the texture.

I remember my parents tried to make me eat one when I was a kid, when I was three, and I threw up violently. Apples, grapes, you name it; I just can't physically swallow it without gagging. My parents though I was going to be in trouble, health wise, having no fruit.

They thought I was going to have bad skin or have some serious repercussions, but it turns out I was fine. We never went to the doctors when I was child because nothing happened to me in result of me not eating fruits. I would say I overcompensated with eating more vegetables but that's a lie. But fruits are high in sugar and funnily enough, they cause digestive problems if consumed at a high rate. I think the best fruits to eat are berries because they are the lowest in carbs, not sure about the sugar levels though. Runners tend to eat fruit a lot, it's good source of energy. The most common one is ironically, bananas. I wouldn't be caught dead eating one. I would rather crawl through a cesspit of rats naked then eat a banana. Well, maybe not - but it would be a close contest.

However, I needed to endure four miles of this. Round and round Palmer Park we go.

I pushed on; I had no choice. Giving yourself no choice is the key to succeeded. Of course, I could stop and run later, or just run back home now and go to the toilet, but you need to allow no other option but to finish the task at hand. Obstacles happen all the time; it's just how you deal with it. The worst part came when I was on the home stretch because I was getting closer. It was like that 29th minute on the treadmill; your mind knows you're about to finish so your body is preparing itself.

I got to the fifth lap and made my way to the exit. I kept vigilant of the huge puddle that was there yesterday - it had evaporated a bit, but it was still vast. The tree wasn't protecting me from the rain now as I exited the park. The trees did their job; now it's time for the home stretch. The rain had got heavier now to add to this dramatic process, I couldn't tell if it did just get heavier or because I wasn't running under the trees anymore. The rain is the least of my worries right now and it wasn't even concerning me for most of the run.

When I got to mile 6.7, I couldn't believe I had held on this far. Reaching 6.7 miles, whilst doing my usual route got me to the flat - but I had to run past it for a bit and then back, to make up that extra 0.3 miles. That was cruelty.

Am I going to get a new challenge like this every day now? I'm taking a beating here, first yesterday with the rain and now today with the rain and the toilet situation, but I did it. That's what I have to take away from this, that I did it, despite those hindrances.

The seven miles was done but I was in no mood to celebrate right now. I wasn't faffing around with doing an extra 0.1 mile or anything like that, I needed to go to the toilet right now!

I got to the flat in the most slapstick way possible, luckily no one was there watching. The second I stopped; I was dying.

My stomach was ready to explode. Keys rattling everywhere, headphones half over my head, water dripping was every part of my face. I crashed through the front door, probably denting the wall that stops it, and of course: Fran is in the bathroom. I saw that little light under the closed door. Fucking typical. I was fuming. She is notoriously known for taking hours in there - well anywhere, for that matter.

While I was kicking my shoes off, which were drenched, I heard one of the greatest sounds ever whilst holding my ass: the toilet flushing.

I let my feelings known, *Fran, I need the toilet or I'm going to shit on this here carpet.*

She still took bloody twenty seconds, even after I said that, but she eventually made her way out, half asleep I might add. I stormed in, with my dripping wet clothes and my shoes in god knows what formation on the shoe rack, my headphone still around my neck, my Relive App still asking if I want to save my video, and god knows what else.

I sat on the toilet and in five, ten seconds, I was alive again. I was in heaven. The liberation was just magical.

It had dawned on me that this was a new part of my journey. Not really thinking about the run but about the destination: the toilet.

I made a side note not to eat katsu curry or large amounts of rice until I've finished this damn challenge. Or better yet, wake up early and squeeze it out. Just jump up and down for a while. God almighty, what a morning this has been.

Has my morning started; I was sat on the toilet thinking about how I even managed to do that run with the pain I was having in my stomach? All of it was gone. But I remembered how it felt, every single inch of that run, how one evil trumped the other.

The second half of this challenge was giving me some real hard hits, but I've managed to get up both times. I need to start throwing some punches of my own now.

1) The focus should always be the destination; the goal is everything. Today, with this false obstacle, it allowed me to open my mind even more. Yes, I needed to go toilet desperately and all my focus was on that. The run, eluded me, the rain eluded me because my grit and focus were so strong because I needed to hit my goal, which today, was going to the toilet. Keep your eye on the prize and you will get there.

2) Having no choice can be a burden when you're not in control of it, but if you're strong enough, you can also have no choice, by eliminating all the other choices yourself. Like, boasting online about doing something, that you now must do, or taking two days off back-to-back, so you have no choice but to complete the run every day without a rest.

3) You can have an obstacle while in another obstacle and it just shows how one of them isn't really an obstacle. The rain wasn't an issue that day because it was trumped by my need to go to the toilet. It could have been sunny, and the same thing would have happened. Sometimes, you need to look back and realised, it wasn't an obstacle but just something different that I wasn't used to. Accepting it is the strongest way to get through it.

7

Clothing

When you watch the pros playing a sport – let's take tennis - you see headbands, wristbands, specific shorts to hold the tennis ball, a top that can breathe. You see Andy Murray wear supports on his ankles, you see Federer tape up certain fingers, and sometimes you see Nadal in a vest top. And yet all you really need is a racket.

Logically, you want to wear shorts, a t-shirt and some trainers. Running is fairly simple - you can run in whatever you want. Wear a tuxedo or a dress, jeans, a leather jacket; because realistically you can run in them. Now a lot of people spend a lot of time choosing the accessories for one of two reasons: either procrastinating on doing the run or the sport, or to semi-commit to doing it. Everything in life is trial and error. Some people can run with headphones, some just can't. Some people need a specific trainer to run in, others can just run in any old trainer.

Once again, it's what's best for you. You will notice, once you take running semi-seriously, that you will be wearing what most runners will wear. There are certain variations - a headband maybe or gloves during the night-time runs - but when it comes down to it, all you have to do is put one foot in front of the other. The rest really doesn't matter. For me, it was a lot of trial and error. The wrong shoes, cotton tops, three quarter length trousers - but now I know I'm more comfortable in breathable shorts and a breathable top. My general rule when running is the most important equipment begins at the bottom of your body and it gets less important the higher you go up your body.

Just my rule. What will yours be?

8
My shoes

Of course, I knew I was going to be in pain, I had just run 8 days in a row, and I had clocked in 58.8 miles. Maybe it was my new trainers? Maybe that's why I was aching? Well, my feet felt fine. I was reading yesterday before bed that the average exercise life for running shoes is six-hundred and forty-four kilometres. How they worked that out, I don't know. What they mean by exercise life is until they are deemed unsuitable to run in. Holes, faded away soles, tread. Any of those determine the factor for a trainer's exercise life.

If successful, I would be running three hundred and twenty-one kilometres, so just over half of this exercise life. I would have used half of my new trainers' exercise life in one month. I'm sorry trainers, but a job has to be done and you're the F1 Car, you're the snooker cue, you're the goalkeeper's gloves, you are the tennis racket. You are the key to helping me succeed.

9

Injuries

When I dislocated my shoulder, I had no control, and it destroyed me. It was the first time in my life I wasn't in control of my limbs and it's a scary feeling - manageable, but scary.

Like anything that takes a physical toll on your body, there are two very simple things to make sure you always do: hydrate and rest. I aim to follow the standard work ethic that works for the rest of society: work for five days and off for two. That's a good guideline but sometimes you do need to push the limits; you do need to raise the bar. I'll tell you something - if you stop because you're not feeling great, then how will you ever find your limits? Pain should be taken advantage of, but always remember: listen to your body.

I knew I had a very vigorous month coming up and, in my head, I had one day off - and that sure wasn't going to be after five days, it was to come after fourteen. So I had to take care of my body. Ice baths, sleeping for eight hours, always keeping hydrated. Simple things that will make all the difference.

Running can be brutal on your body over time - you will hear of things like shin splints, stress fractures or something called Runner's knee, and you will be lucky if you avoid all three throughout your journey into running. But create a balance, Look after yourself. Put a cool pack on your knees, and make sure to stretch. I didn't sustain a serious injury for the first thirty years of my life, and up until then, I thought I was invincible. Sorry to break this to you: no one is. What an individual can be is resilient and driven, and those individuals will take every precaution they can to go above the bar. Utilise the physical pain, take advantage of it, and break barriers. Some runners go until they throw up, some fighters don't give up until they lose consciousness, F1 Drivers lap the circuit seventy-eight times, knowing they have a twenty-five percent chance of dying if they maintain their high average speed. You have to do what it takes. But always remember: to be able to go to that level, you need to make sure to minimise your risk. You need to get to the top in one piece.

10
The second day

The pain of waking up in the early hours of the morning is probably one of the worst feelings in the world. The only time it may be worth doing that, in a general aspect, is when you're waking up to go on holiday and you have that buzz, that three am shower, that drive to the airport in pitch black with no souls or cars out there. It's exciting and you want to get up. This was the mind set I needed to somehow tap into to get me through - and the thing is, anyone can do it. It's about forcing yourself into it, way before your mind can talk yourself out of it. It may not be an attractive holiday with sandy beaches and a piña colada in your hands, but the reason I was getting out of bed for was far more important, and in the longer run, far more rewarding.

I was pushing myself to achieve something worthwhile and, whilst tough moments come with the territory, that should bring a smile to my face, it should make me feel ecstatic. Well on this day, that was certainly not the case. My legs were fucking killing me, and I had had next to no sleep. My eyes were open, but only slightly. The bed of course, was nice and warm. Fran was still asleep next to me, radiating her body warmth and pulling heavily on my envious mind. My jealousy of how peaceful she looked; how comfortable she looked. Not a worry in the world.

It was still mildly dark outside, but the birds were singing, the cars were moving, so the world was already up. Not all of them - in fact, the majority, like Fran, were still in bed, but I needed to get myself moving and out of this bed and ready to tackle the day head on. I couldn't afford to think about anyone else. No more distractions. Well, I lie - part of the beauty of waking up really early is knowing you're up before anyone else, ready to kick-start the day. It doesn't usually work the other way round. People stay up late all the time and if anything, it only attracts negative mental stress the following day. The hypocrite that I am, we were up till 12.15 the night before watching a movie.

I had to get up at six because it took me roughly twenty minutes to fully wake up, brush my teeth, because I like tasting my fresh breath when I run, do my press ups, three sets of thirty, and get my mind pumped, which means choosing which film to play on my run. The run would take me between one hour and one hour ten minutes to complete, which I established with my time the day before, one hour four minutes. This is what I had planned, however my ego tried to get in the way knowing I could run it in fifty-five minutes to an hour, but I needed to make sure my body could endure this for possibly thirty days straight. If anything, I should have been aiming for one hour ten minutes and twelve seconds but hey, let's just take it one day at a time.

I chose *Psycho* as the running movie for day two. The soothing voice of Anthony Perkins as Norman Bates always gives me a sense of enthusiasm, because of the perfect casting done by Hitchcock.

Anyways, according to my plan I would usually make it back home around 7.20 to 7.30 am. Showering and getting ready normally took me twenty minutes mainly because when I was in the shower, I would be lying down in the tub with my phone so I could cool off. I would angle the shower head so I could be on my phone and stretch my legs whilst cooling off at the same time, all of course without getting my phone wet. The only thing I would be doing on my phone was editing my video so it could fit the fifteen second story on social media. My Relive app draws a 3D map of where I just ran, so I can cut it down from thirty-five seconds to fifteen seconds, usually by speeding up a section of the clip and trimming the end, or sometimes I just screenshot the breakdown and added that to the end of the video on Splice.

When I was done with the editing, I would stand up and have a shower and, in that moment, I would feel amazing. Washing all that sweat off, knowing I just ran seven miles. Then out the shower and into my shirt and trousers by 7.40 am. After I would eat breakfast, a cup of coffee was usually there waiting for me thanks to Fran, and then I'd relax for thirty-five minutes while thinking about the run with the news in the background, usually relaying information about COVID-19.

However, as you know, things don't always go according to plan, as much as you want it to. You see, you always budget for an idea of a plan, a sort of breakdown on how the day should go, however, it never usually goes entirely according to your plan. So, as you may have guessed, I completed the run. Day two was okay, no different from the day before in terms of fitness, but more about mental realisation. I had run the path that I was going to run for the next twenty-nine days and today, there was nothing new about the route. As much as day one was hard because it was the first time, I ran seven miles, day two was equally hard, simply for the fact that I had already run it and the surprise of it had worn off. Meaning, I had to dig deep to complete the run today.

Now when finishing a long-distance run, whether it's five miles or twenty-six miles, you should never stop and stand, you should always keep moving, gradually slowing down and then walking it off to catch your breath. So, like I said, that did not go to plan.

I had got back into the flat and I was feeling sick, weak, and just downright awful. The first day was fine - and what I mean by that is that I was feeling great after the run and I was in good nick. However, as I was walking back to the flat on day two, catching my breath and cooling down, something was off. By the time I got into the bathroom, I couldn't even muster up the energy to go on my phone let alone upload my running video on social media. I was feeling sick and it was definitely something new. I didn't have this when I ran a hundred and ninety-six days straight, so something was wrong. Was it the lack of sleep? Was it the stress of knowing I had to do this run? Fucking *Cellular*. I knew I shouldn't have watched it.

This day should have felt like an achievement and it was, it was two days in a row I ran seven miles, but at what cost. Once I got out the shower, I got ready, went into the kitchen and I confided in Fran. I told her if I felt like this today, how was I going to continue for another twenty-eight days? She had already made me coffee and offered me some kind words, she even told me I didn't have to do it, but that ship had sailed. I had to dig deep but it didn't make any sense. Why was I feeling so lightheaded? I was convinced it was the lack of sugar, so I had a bite of a Hershey bar but still nothing, a little better but nothing.

So, I did what most people do these days when something goes south, I Googled it. And thank God I did because I found the answer. I made one mistake that morning, whilst I was thinking about films and trying to wake up, I forgot to do one really important thing. I didn't sip any water the day before.

I looked it up and I had nausea, which is caused by not drinking enough - basically I was dehydrated. I had no water in my body for ten to eleven hours. I had made a mental note not to consume anything after nine pm the night before, which includes caffeine or food, but not water. The day before when we were watching *'Cellular'*, I doubted I had any water although I always have a water bottle on my bedside. Apparently, your intestines get a little tangled when you're dehydrated and it takes a few hours to return to normal. This was a very common symptom for ultra-marathon runners in fact. I just had to ride it out and learn from my mistake. Of course, I was a lot slower than the day before, but I couldn't think about that now. The second day was completed.

As I sat down at the dining room table before leaving for work, I edited and uploaded my running video from my Relieve App. I chose 'Eye of the Tiger' that day. My head wasn't thinking about the song, so I mindlessly went to the most stereotypical running song ever.

As I sat, I took a few deep breaths. I thought about my run and how quick it goes in your head after you've done it but how slow it is when you're doing it. I was slowly recovering from the nausea.

Once I found out the reason behind my fatigue and dizziness, I drank some water when I was uploading my video. Lesson learnt. Mistakes - I always welcome them because it means that mistake is out the way now and I will never make it again. Drink water before a run, so simple.

By the time I got back from work, I had a sort of second wind, and I felt great. I could have gone for a run again - however, I was just getting ahead of myself. It's so true what they say about pain. Pain is just temporary. The thing in my head at that moment was that I was not looking forward to the day after, and it wasn't because of the run, it was because of the pain endured during the run and more importantly, the thought of it.

The worst part of going on a roller coaster is waiting to go on it. Your fear attacks you and you have to fight it. Once you're on it, it's a good feeling, even though it's scary. The lead up to the day after a run was me queuing up again, knowing what to expect. The run may not be Nemesis Inferno but it was still a ride I had to get on.

It's amazing the things you can learn from each day, and the point of doing new things and new challenges, is to simply learn. When stuck in a routine, you know it backwards so it's very hard to learn anything different. That being said, if you're reading books and watching documentaries, and that's part of your routine, then that can further your mind by expanding your viewpoint and knowledge. I love reading books now. Another thing, during lockdown, that people started to do more of. Maybe lockdown wasn't all that bad.

The point is you learn a lot a more from yourself, about yourself and about things revolving around you to make you a better version of yourself. But tomorrow, is tomorrow. You must be present. I had done my run then and it was over with. So, I wanted to enjoy the day and recover in a good fashion ready for the next.

As the day went on, I started relaxing more, I started not to waste my energy too much thinking about the next day. The relaxing feeling was, however, somewhat cut short. Remember, it doesn't matter how much you plan for a day, it doesn't always pan out as you planned.

We all may have our personal battles but let's not get carried away with them. With the right mind set, they can be overcome and only you have the power to do this. What did I learn on this day? Go to sleep early and drink water. Simple things that just needed to nudge me, and the reason I learned them was because I was prepared to make a mistake. Making mistakes is never a bad thing; just make sure you learn from them.

1) Don't be afraid to make mistakes. It's the key to learning.

2) Doesn't matter how much you plan; you should always be prepared for it to deviate from the planned path.

3) Always drink a sip of water before bed. In fact, just consistently drink water throughout the day.

11

It's not over until it's over

The number three has always been an appealing number for me. I think most big numbers are redundant when running - I mean, how often will you come across the number 546?

Three, however, is relevant to everyday life, to establishing patterns, to discovering the odd one out. So, by running this third day, I will have created a pattern with my running, to see if I feel sick like I did yesterday or feel fine like I did on day one. It's like flipping a coin three times to see which side overcomes the other.

That being said, today's run was going to be different from the last two, in terms of time. I was going to run this one in the afternoon, and I knew that yesterday morning, meaning I slept better and yes, I had that sip of water. I planned for a day off work midweek, so I knew after the second day I would be able to lie in and have breakfast before, which would fuel me for this run - so if anything, this should be the easiest run yet. That was the plan anyway. It should have been the simplest and it should have been my quickest. I once heard a good tip; I'm not sure whether it's true or not, but it has logic to it. So here it goes: if you ever want to lose weight and lose it in the speediest, healthiest way, do some cardio the second you get up. Well, not the second you get up, but before having anything to eat.

I did this for the first two days, so that was sort of the downfall of choosing to run in the early morning. I was still sticking to it though. The second day, as you know, I didn't even have any water. I learned that lesson.

When you do cardio in the morning, your body is looking for energy, so it goes straight to its reserves, i.e. your fat - therefore you burn pure fat. There is no carb or sugar for your body to get energy from. So, your body is digging deep, really deep, and you can feel that lactic acid pumping. The feeling of pain and sharp intense jabs inside of you.

It's why morning workouts are better, harder, and more effective. Now for me, yes, I've put on a little bit of weight during lockdown, but I also have twenty-seven days ahead of me to finish this challenge.

My old training instructor from Basingstoke, Richard, sent me his video with several tips about my June challenge, and one of the things he advised was to eat a lot, because I'd be burning over a thousand calories a day with each run.

Well, eating a lot has never been a problem, so I felt good about that.

I had a bowl of porridge and a bagel for breakfast on day three, had a good eight-hour rest, and waited exactly two hours before going running, so my food could go down. The day was nice. Not too hot and with a pleasant breeze: perfect running conditions.

Before I set off, I was killing time on my phone whilst listening to the news, which was shooting back and forth between spikes of coronavirus cases, and the Black Lives Matter protest developing around the world.

I checked my phone and started reading about the charity I had chosen to raise money for, East African Playgrounds. I had made the decision on 31st May, a day before my challenge was set to start. Remember I said my friend told me to do this for charity? Well, I hadn't given any thought about that before so, naturally, I didn't have a charity in mind. I browsed through a list of charities and one popped out to me. It was a picture of a child just smiling up at me while running. I thought that if there was ever a sign, this was it, and I should take a look at this charity. The stories were remarkable. The charity raises money to build playgrounds for kids in East Africa. There isn't much to play with in East Africa besides marbles and guns - and when I say marbles, I mean rocks. We used to play with marbles in Mauritius when I was a kid, and I recall it being fairly enjoyable. That is perhaps my earliest memory of being fairly competitive while playing.

The game is simple and, if you haven't played it before, it more or less goes like this: after digging a hole in the dirt, you take fifteen steps back, draw a line in the dirt, and then throw the marble from behind the line to try and get it in the hole you just dug. Oh, how we entertained ourselves before technology.

The charity's goal is to build swings, parks and general playground facilities, so kids can have a joyful playing experience. I remember reading an article about the journey the children go through just to get to school.

There was this one girl who would walk 8.5 miles to get to her school - it could have been five miles, but to avoid rape and robbery and possible death, she took the long way. She was twelve years old. It was horrible and she was doing the trip twice, there and back, so that was seventeen miles a day. Why the fuck was I complaining about doing seven miles? She did her trip with flip flops that were torn to shred. Her obstacles were not mental battles, but potential physical injury, trauma or, worse, death, and she did this every day, just for an education in hopes of a better life.

I immediately knew that this was the charity I wanted to raise money for, to give those kids a safe space, a bit of happiness when they came back from school, so they could play like kids should. It was small but it may just put a smile on their face, and sometimes that makes all the difference, to have something to look forward to, no matter what it is or how small it is. I recalled this moment of enthusiasm and intensity and raw determination when looking at the charity on the last day of May. I needed to reignite this heat, use it, so that it could fuel me to hopefully make a difference. I saw that I raised £130 by then and I was only three days in. My target was a hundred pounds. I was so pleased, and so I stuck it on my story on social media and tagged the charity.

On the first day I opened my JustGiving page, my friend Chris donated twenty-five pounds. He pushed me to do the challenge for charity, so I have him to thank. It's amazing what a little push can do. It can open doors and give you a different perspective. Always push yourself and others, but do it gently and with care.

It was time to set off. Usually when doing a half marathon or a long-distance run, you should allow a two-to-three-hour gap after you eat. As I was only doing seven miles, I decided to start two hours after my porridge and bagel. Getting in the right mind-set is everything. You also want to avoid running during or near noon because that's when the sun is at its peak - but today was actually quite refreshing, it was cool. After realising this, I put my trainers on and got going.

My pace was evidently quicker on this day. The water, the sleep, the mind-set were all in my favour. All three ticked off the list. I also had the energy from my breakfast that should carry me throughout the run. It doesn't matter if you know it might not carry you - persuading yourself that it may is everything. You just need to trick your mind, and that stops those mental battles when you're running. The more time that passes, the more chance your mind will attack you. That's why the marathon is so hard. Your mind will tell you to slow down, to stop running, and you will fight yourself. On this day I came out blasting and I felt great. I had to slow myself down, because I could see that my pace was getting quicker, and I was comfortable with it. I had twenty-seven days ahead of me; I needed to be efficient.

By lap five of the park, which generally brings me to 5.5 miles, I could see I was on course for running the full distance in under an hour. I was doing the maths in my head and I worked out I needed do the next mile in eight minutes flat - but I didn't. I was wise, and I controlled my pace. Another tip from Richard was not to worry about the time, just focus on staying injury free. Come day twenty-nine or thirty, I will blast an afternoon session, go out with a bang, and smash a time under one hour.

I finally completed the run and I felt incredible, in complete contrast to the day before - I was ready to enjoy the rest of my day off. It was my quickest time, one hour one minute and forty-four seconds. It was then I set myself a challenge within a challenge: to beat this time at some point during my thirty-day challenge. I knew it was only going to get tougher, but I couldn't think of that then. Enjoy the mini victories; they are so significant.

Day three was behind me now and I could rest up ready for the next run. Best feeling in the world is finishing the run and knowing you have remained consistent for at least a few days, especially three. Anyone can go out running, but I had to keep going and keep this momentum going. Of course, day four would be back to be an early morning run, meaning up at 6.10am with nothing in my stomach, and that was looming over in my mind. I had to do seven miles in the morning again because I had work. You must always get in the right mind-set. Always.

I chose 'Lost but Won' as my song to play alongside my video on social media. It was a Hans Zimmer track for the movie 'Rush', great film about the rivalry between F1 Champions Niki Lauda and James Hunt. I finally got to hear Anthony Perkins' voice in 'Psycho' during my run. That was probably another contributing factor to my positive run, actually hearing his superb acting. The day before I think I got to six miles before I even heard him mutter his first syllable; it was annoying and that probably added to the dreadful run I had. Well, no, it was the water, but I can blame it on that too. As the film finished on day three, I still had another mile to go, so I stuck that Hans Zimmer track on, which is about five to six minutes long and it really drove me hard at the end.

The end is always the hardest. When you run a half-marathon, which is thirteen miles, you have a moment of cruise control, but when you get to mile twelve you must really dig deep. In fact, when you get to mile ten, that's when the real endurance and determination come in. You need to find another gear. It doesn't matter how far you're running, whether it's 5k or seven miles, that last kilometre or that last mile will be difficult simply because you know it's about to finish. Your body instinctively listens to your head and starts shutting down, so it gets harder. If you let it, it will bring you down to your knees.

Always treat the end with respect. I'd watched a documentary a while back about the french man who tight-roped between the Twin Towers with no safety net, Phillipe Petit. He accomplished it back in 1974. There was a film made about it around six years ago with Joseph Gordon-Levitt in it - I think it was called "The Walk".

Anyway, the documentary shows that when he was a kid, he had a mentor who taught him how to tight-rope. I think the mentor worked in a circus. After he taught him and thought he was ready, he removed the safety net and told him to walk the line, to remove fear, stay focused and be confident in doing the walk - and Phillippe did it!

He got all the way to the very end; he had one step left and was about to step off the rope - and then he simply lost focus because he was at the end and almost fell.

The lesson he learned that day was to always stay focused. Yes, the worse was probably over, but it didn't matter if he was inches away from the edge or in the middle; you have to remain focused regardless of how close or how far you may be. When he did the famous walk in 1974 across the Twin Towers, 1368 feet high, he almost repeated the same mistake again; but his focus was so strong because he learned his lesson at the circus. He stayed vigilant.

Just because you're close to finishing, it doesn't mean you're there yet. Always push past the line and only then can you drop the focus. The same applies when you're running, when you hit that twelfth mile during the half marathon or the twenty-fifth mile in a marathon or even the four kilometre in a 5k race. Don't focus on it almost finishing - continue your drive and keep doing what you're doing. It's not over until it's over.

Needless to say, that's why I put on that specific track, because it pressed me to finish the seven miles as I'd set off to do - and, truth be told, it was great to hear dramatic music for a change rather than people chatting in a film, although that still takes my mind away from the pain.

Another good thing about having a day off is taking your time to do things. The reason I was uploading my Relive videos in the shower was to save time. Always make sure you're efficient with your time. One hour of each of my days in June was going to be running; then I would have to recover, shower, download, edit, upload, and work on raising money for charity. So, I would usually do all of it at the same time - but this day, because I had no work, I was in no rush. I was just sat in my trackies uploading my third run. Day three was a wonderful day. Compared to the disaster that was day two, it was a very good day. Best day yet.

That's ten percent of my challenge done. Numbers become essential when doing things like this.

Like I said, big numbers tend to be unnecessary when running. They are there for added value or to emphasise an achievement, but doing three of something determines a pattern, and today, after my third run, I liked what I was seeing.

The trick is to always enjoy the present, but in this personal challenge of mine it was very hard to do that without thinking about the next day. The hours were counting down until reaching 6am again when I would have to do this all over again. That night, I reassured Fran that I was fine, that day two had been a learning curve and with anticipation, I had a found some sort of consistent routine now and began developing a pattern.

1) Establish and look out for patterns.

2) Enjoy the mini victories.

3) Sometimes people, including yourself, need a little push.

12

Snooze

It doesn't matter how much you persuade yourself to get in the right mind-set, something will always trip you up. And it's generally something fairly minor. Sometimes your mind, no matter how strong you think it may be, just doesn't want to fall in line.

After giving myself a nice little pep-talk the night before, I thought I was ready for day four; I was ready to smash it. I had my alarm on, as per usual, at six o'clock and was ready to get out there and try and duplicate my efforts from the day before. I was contemplating changing my alarm tone to something more upbeat but then, whatever that upbeat song or tune may be, you just begin kind of relating that tune to an alarm and that ruins it. It just reminds you every time you hear it of those early mornings and no one wants to be reminded of that.

It always takes something small to take you off course. The smallest wrench can jam the whole mechanism of the Big Ben clock. It only takes something tiny to challenge something big, which is why stability and effort are so crucial to achieving tasks, projects and more significantly, personal goals.

Now, granted, I had gone to bed at 11.30pm, but that was still six and half hours of sleep. However, I Googled it and, according to a university study, the body declines in function if you don't have seven to eight hours' sleep. I call bullshit on that, but I didn't have the time to be ignorant because what I did, what was about to affect my whole routine here, was to stupidly put my alarm on snooze. That was all I did. The small wrench has made its impact, now for the repercussions.

You give yourself a big speech the night before, convincing yourself you will get up early and do this and that - and yet when the time comes, your body just doesn't want to be disturbed. My body was not having any of it. But these are the moments that I needed to look forward to. You want these moments. Overcoming something hard is what it's all about.

My alarm rang, and I smashed my phoned with my hand. I say smash; I just half-consciously flung my arm to snooze the alarm. The noise was unbearable. I have no idea why on this day it was particularly excruciating - maybe the last three days had caught up on me.

I snoozed it. Of course, that was a mistake. For the first three days my alarm had rang, and whilst, yes, I struggled to get up, I did wake up.

Day four was another thing all together. I was still half asleep, and I didn't want to be disturbed, in spite of my pep talk to myself the night before and knowing, full well, I had to do this. The last three days must have worn me down. The twenty-one miles I had run, the mental strains I had been going through, adjusting to this new routine.

Doctors always say to listen to your body. I've been a firm believer in that, particularly when I dislocated my shoulder - but when doing something like this, something extraordinary, you need to reconsider some things. When you're doing something different, something that is going to really confront you, you need to start listening to your mind and trying to flood out all the naysayers. People telling you two-hundred miles is impossible; your legs will get destroyed, your knees will fail, all this stuff.

Never listen to anyone but yourself, and if you're wrong, then be ready to accept the consequences and learn from it. I knew I could do it - the doubt was just laziness. If I can move, I can walk and if I can walk, I can run. If I can wiggle my big toe, I should be okay.

I'm thirty years old and I'm about to run two-hundred miles; these are just numbers, but numbers become your best friend when you're alone doing these physical challenges. I don't care what people say I can or cannot do. I can and will do this. My body might be exhausted, but I can do this.

My alarm snoozed three more times. I finally woke up properly at 6.40am. I would have been on the second mile by then if I had stuck to the schedule from the previous three days. I would have done my press ups, I would have brushed my teeth, got dressed, had that very important sip of water, and I would have been two miles in.

That is how important time is. Look how much time I lost, simply because I stayed in bed an extra thirty to forty minutes. The realisation was that I still had to run. I couldn't talk myself out of it - I didn't have that luxury. Why did I do this for charity? Why did I tell everyone? If I hadn't done that, could I have cheated? No, I couldn't live with that. But there would have been an option there to give up without anyone knowing. A very tempting alternative.

I finally got up and I started to think. When I say get up, I sat on the edge of the bed. I looked at my phone and saw the time and I just felt low - but I was up, at least that was one thing. Time is one thing that just keeps going, it doesn't wait for anything. Time is such a luxury and maybe I needed to learn that again. It's okay to learn the same thing twice.

I needed to get off the bed. I really needed to get up. If I ran seven miles, let's say in one hour to one hour and ten minutes, and I got out of bed right then, did my press ups, brushed my teeth and got ready, I would be done by eight-ish. I had work at nine. I wouldn't have time for breakfast, which was fine, but more essentially I would have broken my routine. But I had to come to terms with this new plan.

There and then, I made a decision, and it was something Richard told me to do. I decided to split up my runs and, to my surprise, it brought a little smile to my face.

I would run half the distance now and half of it when I get back from work. It wasn't ideal but I knew I would have to do that at some point during my thirty days. This is a lesson to learn. And when it comes to moments like these, you need to adapt to the situation at hand.

I woke up late and now I needed to tackle this task in an alternative way. I woke up and I did my press ups. I did them quicker. I did them really quick. Three sets of thirty. In between the first two sets, I brushed my teeth. Between the second and third, I got ready and put my headphones on. I didn't select a film, I just stuck Spotify on. No time.

I was out the door at 6.55am. Before seven. That was a mini accomplishment for me. Remember, take every victory you can get. When I was running, I knew I wasn't doing the whole seven miles, which was refreshing. I was loving it. But I couldn't get too attracted to this otherwise it may have become the new routine. I had spent three days getting up at the right time to do seven miles in one go. Now the downfall to the new routine, which was already looming over my head, was that I would have to run at least 3.5 miles once I get back from work.

At least I would have had breakfast and lunch by then, so I would have the fuel for that run - it should be nice and easy, and I was just going to focus on running 3.5 miles when the time came, not now. Although by the time I got back from work and started running the other half, I would have kids and other runners around, as well as traffic.

This was why I needed to get up early. Maybe I should have gone Fred Flintstone and use a coconut dropping on my head as an alarm. Not sure that would be safe though.

By mile two, I was cruising, and it was becoming a nice jog. I was enjoying it and part of me was thinking: maybe this isn't all bad, not exerting myself with seven miles in the morning, spacing it out instead. Richard said that a bit of variety is good, it mixes things up a little, and since I had already decided I was not going to change the route, I thought this was the next best thing. Although not according to plan, I adapted, and here we were.

I felt like this should have been a punishment for not getting up on time, but truth be told, I was enjoying the shorter run, knowing, in my mind, that I didn't have to run the full seven miles. The thought of that consumed me for a while and I accidently started a third lap of the park by routine, but I exited on Wokingham Road, which was the entrance I had come in from, and began to make my way back.

It worked out to be 4.4 miles and I was back around half seven. Less sweaty, with more energy and over half the run done and then it hit me. As I was showering and uploading, I realised, the job wasn't done yet. I couldn't celebrate just yet. Yes, okay, I only had to run 2.7 miles, but it just meant that little thing nagging at you for the rest of the day. The day was certainly not done yet.

It's about biting the frog. An old saying; I believe it comes from Mark Twain. He says that if you wake up and the first thing you do is eat a live frog, then you can go through the rest of the day knowing the worst is behind you. That's why running seven miles in the morning meant a lot. It was my frog. Everyone has their own frog. What I did today was eat the body and the head and left the arms and legs till later. Using the frog analogy is even more emphatic for me, because out of all the creatures on earth, frogs creep me out the most. There's just something about them that really creeps me out. I'll never forget that line from the film Cool Runnings: "We're different. People are always afraid of what's different." Yes, well that rings true. But frogs are slimy and have crazy eyes and are bizarrely small, and in fact they are the most poisonous animal in the world, so my fear has some logic. However, those poisonous frogs are in South America and I'm lying to myself, as the look of them is the primary reason why I don't like them.

Spinning off topic here. My day carried on as normal; I uploaded my video and went to work. As you can guess, work was a little different, with the knowledge that I had to still go running. This also meant that the gap and rest time between the next run and the previous would be shorter. I finished work at 5.30pm. One decent thing about the lockdown was traffic, more specifically at rush hour: there wasn't that much. It was easy to drive around, particularly if you live in Reading. Because of that, petrol prices were also cheap, cheapest they have been in years.

It took me fifteen minutes to drive back home without that traffic, two minutes to change from my work gear into my running gear, and then away I went again. With traffic, it's double the amount.

You know how I said running without stopping was one of my OCDs, where I had to make sure I wouldn't stop? Well, here's another one. I couldn't run less than three miles. I had to run at least three miles, but three miles doesn't get me to my flat and back in a nice fashion. Even with two laps of the park and jogging back to my flat from the Wokingham Road exit, that would clock around 3.4 miles. So, in my head, that was what I was going to do, and that extra 0.4 would be vital for later on in the month. In the end, it wasn't such a bad thing once I started doing it. That rings true for most things. We spend most of the time worrying about something for no reason. I had a realisation on day four, more so than on any of the previous three days, that this whole way of thinking about something you don't want to do, or fear doing, is something we need to explore. Like why did I have this mind-set? Is running universally negative? Is waking up early universally negative? I still haven't figured out this mind-set. It only is negative if you think it is. I just know that I must do it so in my head it becomes like a chore and by thinking like that I end up resenting it.

When I ran the 3.4 miles in the afternoon, yes, there were a lot of cars, there were a lot of people in the park that I had to run around, and this is time I'm spending running when I should be at home resting for the next day. The important thing is always about adapting to a situation and learning from it, perhaps even discovering that it isn't as bad as you thought.

I could have chosen to run three miles and then walk the rest of the way back - but what would have been the point in that? If I'm walking back, I may as well use that distance to contribute to my goal. You see each step is important, no matter how small, and what I realised on this day was that, yes, it doesn't matter how small the step is, and it also doesn't matter how you do it and how you get there, as long as you're moving in the right direction. The whole point of journeys is to learn from them, and, most importantly, to overcome an obstacle with a mentality that continues to drive forward. On this day I did not have a minor setback, I did things differently after what I thought was an obstacle. Sometimes, they are not obstacles at all. They are learning curves, but it's up to you to discover that in your mind-set. I thought I was getting the hang of it then.

Earlier, I said I was being too ignorant when thinking we don't really need seven to eight hours of sleep. Well, I had time then to be a little ignorant. I had just finished my run; it took me thirty minutes to run 3.4 miles and together I had run 28.8 miles in four days. I showered; I edited and uploaded my video, for the second time that day. I grabbed a beer and enjoyed this mini victory; the victory of overcoming what I thought was an obstacle.

Being ignorant is preaching about something usually when you don't have a leg to stand on. Without knowledge, just babbling. Now, who am I to say seven to eight hours is not the right number of hours to sleep? It probably is and it's the recommended time from experts; I can't disagree with the research and science behind it. However, the whole speech about rules are meant to be broken and limits should be pushed is something that has always stayed with me.

How can you know anything until you do it? How do you discover yourself without pushing your limits, without breaking the rules? These things, the recommended sleeping times, are there as guidelines for those who want to have rules, who want a structure, and that is okay - but how can we move forward in uncovering what you might be capable of accomplishing or learning.

This reminds me of a film called "Whiplash" featuring a teacher who pushes and pushes this student to become a better drummer. He abuses him verbally; he hits him a few times and he even hurls a chair at him.

He eventually drops him from the band and humiliates him on stage, with his friends and family watching. Halfway through the film, the teacher explains to the student that Charlie Parker, who was a famous jazz saxophonist, didn't become Charlie Parker because he stuck to the limits that society confined him to. He was pushed. The teacher goes on to say that any untapped potential is criminal, that you may be denying the world of the next Buddy Rich or Einstein, and it happens on a day-to-day basis. At the end, after being humiliated on stage, the student comes back from sulking and recommences playing, and ultimately there is a revelation at the end of the movie that the teacher finally got the best out of him, through all the abuse, the thirteen-hour days of practising and teaching and blood and sweat, the kid went through it and didn't quit. It was quite an excessive lesson, but only excessive to those who are not ready for it.

My point is, do you think Arnold Schwarzenegger or Steve Jobs or Steve Bezos did the things they did by not pushing boundaries? I think boundaries should be pushed if you really are set on doing the best you can, and sometimes the result may just be worth it. It's about the realistic mind-set that stays consistent and using it to do what you can in this lifetime.

Something will trip you up - it happens all the time - but you have to also invite the obstacles in because it is those moments where you enter the unknown and are challenged that force you to adapt and grow. In those moments, it's all about self-discovery. I snoozed my alarm. It happens. You overcome it. You learn. What will your hurdle be? What will trip you up?

1) Don't be afraid to push boundaries. It's about self-discovery.

2) Adapt to the obstacle, don't dwell on it.

3) Make sure to eat your frog nice and early.

13

Breaking routine

Well after a much needed day off, my alarm woke me up at around 6.20am. God, what an awful feeling when you know you have to run seven mile. You figure after nine days, you might get up naturally - but no, that was saved for the days off, when I didn't need to get up. Well, I couldn't dwell on this, I didn't have the time.

The comments and likes from my Facebook post were still coming in from the day before. I even tried to reread it when I got up, but my eyes were still blurry, and I knew I was just distracting myself from the inevitable. I couldn't sit there and do that then; I needed to get out, and I needed to get out there right there and then. It was already quite late, in terms of my routine. It was approaching 6.35am and I hadn't left yet. Time always seems to speed up when you don't want it to. Theory of relativity I guess. You put your hand on a hot woman, an hour can seem like a second. You put your hand on a hot stove, a second can seem like an hour. It's all relative.

Anyways, without procrastinating any further, I just got up and left. Right out the door. I just didn't think about it. I somehow, in my sleep, put my shoes on, got dressed into my Nike gear and stepped outside. That instant, when the cold air hits you, I was awake. It's like splashing water in your face repeatedly.

The birds tweeting, the fresh, cold air on your face, and the sounds of the cars whizzing through London Road in Reading. The run had woken me up for the wrong reasons. I was in pain, but it was similar to most pains you get when you start running so I didn't think much of it - but my mind was really entertaining the pain today. Was I fatigued? Did I hurt myself? I had no idea.

The 7.5-mile run from the day before has drained me, and I was beginning to realise that this challenge was not going to be a walk in the park. Both figuratively and practically speaking. Well, no shit it wasn't. I just thought I would be stronger after eight days.

I had to somehow overcome pain and fight against my mental instability here. Christ, it was only day nine. I approached Palmer Park where I began the first of my scheduled five laps of the park. By the time I reach Palmer Park, it's about 0.7 miles from running from the flat to the park, and on this day it felt like a lifetime. Everything was going wrong. People were in my way, I couldn't cross the road, because of the traffic on London Road, which meant I almost had to slow my pace to nearly a complete stop. Luckily, I managed to keep jogging before coming to a complete stop. That would have put a cross on the whole damn thing.

It just was not a good vibe. I kept telling myself there is always this negative feeling when I run, but I just needed to suck it up. Another annoying thing that was soon dwelling on my mind, was time. Time was against me. Time is against us all, in fact.

I had work at nine and I had set off quite late. I was actually looking for excuses and today on day nine, I had found enough excuses to lap Palmer Park only twice and then return back home, which was the route I would usually do for my runs in May with Fran. This clocked in around 3.7 miles to four miles depending on where I stopped on the long stretch of road back to my flat.

I had already decided when I got to my second lap, that I was heading home after, and I would do the remaining 3.2 miles after work which didn't sound bad. Never does at the time though, does it?

I was both pissed off and relived. My body had beaten my mind. I allowed every fear or excuses in my mentality to take over. My mind set in the morning was wrong and no matter how many times you try to convince yourself to stay focused, you will always face the same mental battles. The fact of the matter is, I did leave the house, and I did run. However, this is something I cannot get used to, especially this early on. Another part of me was saying I failed today.

Obviously the second I finished, my breathing was fine, but my mind wasn't. It's amazing how quickly things can turn around. I had a full eight hours of work in front of me and I was feeling a little sour but hey, it was done. I just needed to run 3.2 miles when I got back which is two laps back and the same route back instead of the longer way back, so it was easy.

After I did that, I would finally be on double figures. I would have done nine straight days and swiftly moving on to day ten.

When I was running half-marathons, they put markers

on every mile you do to signify how far you'd run. A Half Marathon is 13.1 miles. When I saw the tenth marker, it was like Christmas, simply because it was double figures. That's all it took. A subtle indication that you are moving up and these little moments are so important to boosting your drive.

I knew I had no days off until the weekend so I had to make sure I could wake up early and smash out the seven miles every day until then.

I feel like you can never enjoy the present because there is always something there to bring you down, something you don't look forward to. This is why it's so important to have things to look forward to, it doesn't matter what it is or how small it is. It could be a film you haven't seen, or something you've ordered that hasn't arrived yet, or the football restarting.

With lockdown, there were many things to look forward to and I felt in a way, that since we had no football, no restaurants to eat out in, no cinemas to go to, no socialising at parties or nightclubs, or simply having a pint at your local pub, I figured this period should be as hellish as possible. So, when lockdown is finally over, normal life would be ten times better and then you can recount the tales of your misery and struggle during lockdown over a pint at the pub.

We have to embrace the dark times and own it. Yes, things are not normal anymore and things feel like they're up in the air but it's an opportunity to see how you come out of it. To really enjoy something, you have to go through the pain, you have to accept that there is misery before joy. When going for a run, the run itself is the misery for most, and even today for me, it was. However, the second you finish it, it's liberating, you can enjoy it more because you know you've earned it.

You read about Olympians who train for four years for ten seconds but the glory afterwards is worth every single second of those four years and that is what it takes. To be consistent every day, ready for when you can finally celebrate your achievements. I realise what I'm doing is self-inflicted and in a way self-serving however, it's the challenge I've chosen for me to push myself to start this journey of self-discovery.

Planning something and doing something are two completely different things, put them together though and great things can happen. I could have planned more carefully to run two-hundred miles, but with more time passing, I would have probably talked myself out of it. That's why it took me no less than twenty-four hours to make this decision and committing to doing it.

I could have been inside, doing nothing during lockdown and to be honest, lockdown hasn't really changed much for me, I'm still going to work and I'm still doing my own thing but the social aspect has gone and that has created time so I've decided to substitute my pleasure, with pain, well, with a goal, a target and see what happens. It's self-discovery and with self-discovery, comes new territory so you need to be ready for anything.

The second I got back home from work, I didn't waste any time, I stuck my shoes on and went straight back outside. Any seconds wasted would have turned in a minute, which would have turned into a dangerous game of procrastination.

Another thing about breaking routine is sometimes you forget about the really small things that make up your usual routine and today, this small thing managed to hit me right square in the face.

I was just about to jog and before I usually set off, I get my Relive app ready to record and my chosen track or movie ready to play but today, was different. Today was a disaster. Well, that's a little melodramatic but anything small that breaks a routine that you've been carefully following is disastrous.

I saw my battery life on my iPhone. Three percent. Three fucking percent. I may have only been doing 3.2 miles today, but that would still take twenty to thirty minutes whilst my Relive app was recording, with my movie in the background. Well, I guess music now, since that takes less battery, neither would survive for thirty minutes on three percent to be honest.

The app alone would drain away that three bloody percent before I finished my run, let alone sticking a movie on. I had to go back inside and charge my phone.

If there had been something to kick in my general proximity at the time, I would have kicked it. Fuck sake. I had to go back inside and charge my phone and what's more demoralising; I was already in my running gear. I needed to keep my mind strong. Charge your phone, don't get comfortable, just do some stretches and wait for the phone to charge, I figured twenty percent would be enough to survive the run.

I deleted all my history, put my phone on airplane mode, I did everything to make it charge quicker. I was sat quietly on my bed and then I saw a book that I've been meaning to read, Ant Middleton's *First Man*.

A friend of mine recommended it, after she saw what I was doing for charity. Whilst the phone was charging, I decided to read a few pages. A few pages suddenly turned into a few chapters and before I knew it, I had been sat there for twenty minutes on the edge of my bed in my running gear.

My phone read thirty-four percent, and with some mental fuel from *First Man* I stayed focused and returned outside for my run. A slight little obstacle at first turned into nothing more than a push to maybe read a few chapters.

In case you don't know him, Ant Middleton he is a British former soldier who worked in various units with the Army. He now does mental and physical focused programmes on Channel Four and has written four to five books, mainly focusing on how important it is to stay positive and how to get the best out of yourself. A motivational type of book basically. It added fuel to a dying fire.

The beauty about running early in the morning was that it wasn't that busy. You would have others around, some walking their dogs and other joggers coming in towards the second half of my run, but besides them it was quiet. When I say quiet, I mainly mean no children.

That being said though, the 0.7 miles to the park that morning was annoying. No idea why people were up that early. But then I realised it was because I had left around ten minutes later than I usually did, which creates new circumstances.

It's amazing how ten minutes changes everything.

Apparently, there was a Second Officer called David Blair in 1912 and he forgot to hand his keys to a locker that contained binoculars in a room on a cruise ship. He apparently had a five-minute conversation with someone outside the ship before he remembered he had to hand the keys to the cabinet, where the binoculars were. It was too late by then, the ship set sail and if he hadn't talked to that person for five minutes, then the Titanic maybe would not have sank. The crew of the Titanic used only their eyes to look out for icebergs since no one knew where the keys were for the cabinet. In fact, in David Blair's defence, no one knew there were binoculars in that cabinet in the first place. But it just shows how important time can be, and how it could determine outcomes.

If I had woken up ten minutes earlier, I would have been in a good mind set for those 0.7 miles and avoided the traffic and the people getting in my way, and therefore would have been able to continue to run the whole seven miles. Ten minutes, that's all it takes, that's all it took to change my day today. But let's not keep dwelling.

That's all it could take to change your day, that or your battery reading three percent. That was a sucker punch and that's all it can take to me not running in the evening. I stayed strong and thanks to my book, I managed to knuckle down. You see, these moments are key in finding out how you deal with these minor setbacks, these are the moments you want to test yourself. Anyone can do something if they plan it. The only hard bit about it is sticking to it, which means overcoming unnecessary and unpredictable obstacles and that's what separates people.

All I was thinking about when running was Ant's voice in my head. I took the slow route back when I did the evening run, meaning I knew I was not going to do another 3.7 miles in the evening. The short route back meant I would be only be clocking in 3.3 or 3.4 miles. I only had to do 3.2 miles today, so it wasn't a massive tragedy but given my mind set, I thought

I needed to get back as soon as possible and just prepare myself for the week.

That evening, I had little energy left in me and to be fair it wasn't surprising because I had no food in me acting as energy. I made my way back to my flat, checked my phone and realised I had done 3.3 miles which together with the 3.8 that I did in the morning meant I had bagged an extra 0.1 miles and that was the first time, that whole day, I felt positive.

I had done something extra today despite that awful morning start. It had occurred to me that maybe because of work, I should maybe split my runs up until Friday and I secretly wanted to, because I honestly couldn't even think about doing a seven-mile run right then. That would have meant later alarms and less distance. It was also one of my tips by Richard and a few others to maybe just split them up. It was then and there I decided I would split up my runs for the next three runs.

I did ask myself whether I was doing it because I was secretly defeated about doing seven miles. Was I scared?

I had to tread carefully here. In my head I was weighing up the pros and cons. The longer I avoided doing seven miles straight, the more splitting the runs would become the norm. I had to keep my head straight.

Saturday you will be off, I told myself, and you will have the time to smash out seven miles in peace. Nothing peaceful about it usually, but that would be the plan.

The important thing is that I planned. It's okay if you change halfway through, you can adapt to what suits you at the time, but you need to make sure your frame of mind can handle little cracks in your routine and furthermore, when you recommence the old plan, that the transition itself won't bring you down mentally. Another good thing about making this plan was that I knew the day after I would be doing a split. The bit I needed to focus on was that the run would be spread across the whole day now.

Sometimes, you need to break your own rules to see what your mind can take. Remember, this isn't about running, this is about testing what your mind can go through.

1) Being in new territory is both necessary for your mind and body. It allows you to see how you overcome anything outside your comfort zone and this will be beneficial in learning how to cope or handle things not glued to your routine.

2) The smaller parts of your routine is just as important as the bigger ones. Charging my phone is just as important as running seven miles. When a game of chess finishes, the pawn and the queen go back in the same box.

3) Breaking a routine is fine but make sure you have a plan to overcome this break in routine. Routine is just about structure, so in case of sudden cracks it's all about overcoming and improvising.

14

Hobbies

Mental health seemed to me a term that was thrown around at every which circumstance -either as a scapegoat or as an excuse in not being able to perform. Some still think this. As this pandemic took its shape, I realised how ignorant I was being; how people must be getting affected with their own head and the uncertainty of it all. People need each other. People need to be doing things with each other outside of work and that was put to a conclusive halt when COVID-19 hit. That's one thing I've learnt.

Another thing I've discovered is that people just need something to do. The one thing that gives life meaning is death, as callous as that sounds. Our lives come to an end, and so we're knowingly on the clock; we can't just work and sleep all the time, or even spend it accomplishing personal challenges. You have to enjoy this ride, otherwise what's the point on being on it? Imagine being on a roller coaster and just sitting there, emotionless. No matter what tasks you've got ahead of you or that you're doing, what job you do and how strenuous it is, or what demons you're fighting within yourself, always find the time to do your hobby, whatever it may be. I cannot stress that enough, even if it means carving time by sleeping less or working less. They give you an out, they relieve the stress and it just puts a pause on life. It's a time out; it's a part that is crucial. I call it the recharge station and you have to make sure, no matter how driven you are, to find the time to do something you love - your guilty pleasure, your silly pastime, whatever it is.

Do it because it's good for the mind. By keeping yourself engaged with something that makes you happy, you'll have the energy in the long run to tackle work and tasks. It is needed, and it shouldn't be avoided.

15

Films

We were watching *Cellular*. It had a young Chris Evans in it. This was the main reason for my mental battle in getting out of bed. Six hours' sleep because I was watching some movie that I had already seen. What is wrong with me?

See the thing is, Fran hadn't seen the movie. I like educating Fran, or anyone in fact, with films, and what I mean by that is trying to allow them to watch films they normally wouldn't. Now I am not saying people won't watch films like *Citizen Kane* or *Casablanca* - however with my generation, and even the post-millennial one, it's a safe assumption to say they are not going to sit through a three-hour black and white movie made fifty years ago. I mean have you seen *The Godfather* all the way through or *The Deer Hunter?*

Now *Cellular* wasn't exactly Oscar-worthy - it was a light-hearted movie that did the job of keeping my attention for ninety minutes. But it was a film that Fran hadn't watched and the experience in watching a film is everything. People now watch a movie with one hand on their phone, or have it on in the background while they're doing something else. This I cannot allow.

Cinema is slowly dying, and this virus has not made things better. Productions have stopped everywhere, all over the globe. The new James Bond film was supposed to be released in September, then it was pushed back to October and now it's next year. Late next year! People don't even want to go the cinema anymore and this was an issue before COVID-19. People have the luxury of enjoying things in their own homes, skip adverts, and record things they've missed, as well as being spoilt for choice on what to watch on which streaming network. It's a new world now. Back in the day when you watched an episode on TV you'd have to wait until the week after to watch the next episode. In-between that, you would be having conversations with other people who had seen it, and you would talk about last week's episode, and that itself was so much fun but now, it's just too efficient. You can now binge watch whatever you want at any given time.

We have so much power now where we can watch anything we want, and it's become the norm. Now with COVID, people are not going to the cinema, it's just enhancing the fact that films can be enjoyed in your own homes. I heard recently that the new Mulan movie, which was originally going to be released in cinema, is now going straight onto Disney's streaming platform available for an extra fee. They will make a killing if they do that. People just don't want to go to the cinema like they used to anymore. It's slowly fading away, one of many things being eaten up by this virus.

Anyways, as you can probably tell I have an extreme passion for films. I'm one of those annoying pretentious people that like old movies and artsy movies, but my range is broad when it comes to films. I just love the art of visual storytelling. The beauty of sitting through an entire movie just watching it and simply doing nothing else is a lost art now. Watching a film should be an escape but now it's just background noise but it will survive, it just depends on how.

When I was living with my parents, which was for the first thirty years of my life, I would always pick old renowned films when watching TV with my sister so she has me to thank for her high knowledge in cinema. I wouldn't force her to watch them, but when my parents went to bed at nine, my sister and I would have the TV and we would usually watch films that I had recommended or chosen. For someone her age, early teens to mid-twenties, it's easy to fall into reality TV, rom-coms, comfort movies like Adam Sandler or Paul Rudd movies, and they are fine, but what I did with her, subconsciously, is introduce her to the classics and build her appetite on them. Films like *Usual Suspects*, *Psycho*, *Rocky*, *American Beauty*, *Reservoir Dogs*. Of course, we would indulge in your typical blockbuster movie or series every now and again, but early on this is what I did. I helped her watch these movies, or she would have been missing out on pop culture references which are mainly based on quoting old, and more importantly renowned, movies. More significantly than that, I helped her savour the journey of truly experiencing a movie, the message it conveys to you, and the perspective you choose to see it in.

I was speaking to her the other day actually, she's five years younger than me and she's a teacher. We still talk about films to this day and I still always recommend films to her and I find now, she recommends films to me too. Like I said, she's a teacher so we were also talking about how the virus has affected her job.

Lessons at school have now been from their laptops, so my sister is teaching online to a handful of students via Zoom. Another thing that is associated with COVID. Zoom or Teams and all that jazz.

She was telling me all this when I was on the phone to her in May, and it sounded so stressful on her part. Unfortunately, this is just the tip of the iceberg with what's happening with teachers and just education in general, let alone what's happening around the world. It's just too risky to have a classroom full of children and it would be under her responsibility. There's so much on the line there, which creates more stress because you have a main responsibility, children's lives. That is just too much responsibility, but with responsibility, comes growth and character building so it's about embracing the challenge. I'm not in her shoes though and I can't presume what she must be going through just like she can't presume my pain with this fucking run after one day.

So yes, six hours sleep and my love for films. When Fran and I moved in together at the end of January, two months before the shit hit the fan with the world, I basically did the same thing with her. I was doing it anyways and she did it to me too with films I hadn't seen, when I spent the weekends with her in London.

Fran is slowly getting there, and she has a natural taste for good films, but she is still stubborn. Of course, I compromise when she wants me to watch some animated feature, but truth be told, I love all films. I don't really outright reject any film. Yes, I dislike some films, but you can't judge a film by a few scenes, let alone the trailer.

Anyways, *Cellular* was neither a classic nor artsy just a good film Fran hadn't seen it and I simply wanted to share that experience with her. In my head, it was worth it. Well, you know what, when I woke up, no it wasn't worth it. I should have slept for at least eight hours. But it's something to learn from, and that is exactly why we make mistakes, to learn from them.

It was time to get up. All I had been doing was reminiscing about films. I was grumpy and tired and worse off I was procrastinating here. This was day two and I was still in bed. This was harder than I thought it would be. It shouldn't be easy. Nothing worth doing should be. I only had myself to blame for how I felt right then. Fran looked so peaceful in bed, part of me wanted to wake her up because I was being that petty, but I wouldn't. I couldn't. It was extremely tempting though. I got out of bed and my feet touched the floor. I slowly stood up and felt my body get into gear.

16

Football

I promptly put my alarm on the night before even though I knew I was off. The excitement to see what I could do after two days off was burning through me. Breaking routine was treacherous. It was like me taking a different route. It works for some people but not for me. I had to stick to that same route. I knew every inch of it. I knew every jogger out there, the Gurkhas, the dog walkers, the people power walking and by now, they knew me. Probably wondering where I was for the last two days.

After doing my press ups, I put on my freshly washed shorts and stuck my shoes on and stepped outside. My legs were fresh, my phone was fully charged, my headphones were definitely fully charged and I was fully charged.

Whilst charging my phone I realised it was the return of the Premier League and Arsenal were playing. I couldn't wait. Almost hundred days without football. It was some extra fuel in my mind has I was prepping myself to start running.

One-hundred days without football was sinful to me. My weekends, before this challenge, were lacking any real purpose. I would have this routine, way before lockdown, with doing my dream team on the Friday night, watching some of the football, exchanging banter with the lads on WhatsApp about the football - then I would watch Match of the Day in the evening.

It's amazing how we take the minor things for granted. We moved into our flat on January 31st, a day before Frans birthday, so we didn't really get to celebrate properly, with all the madness of moving. Who would of thought, two-three months later, all things we took for granted was coming to an end? No cinema, no restaurant, no socialising.

My weekends had no routine anymore - they would be filled with quizzes and the odd Zoom call now and again. I felt imprisoned, I felt like I had no control, and I didn't. All I wanted to do was find a reason to look forward to the weekend. It was bad of me to think like that, but it was the truth, my weekends were very packed with things to do and a majority of it, was to do with football.

One thing I've learnt is to never take anything for granted, no matter how small it is. The feeling of watching football again, watching Arsenal was extraordinary. I wish people could feel the way I'm feeling today. And I'm sure there are football fans out there, that are feeling like me right now. People have their own personal things to looking forward to when this is all over, like when the restaurants finally open or when we can go see our families.

The longer lockdown prevents us from enjoying the things, we once saw as routine, the more we started to appreciate the little things and I think after this whole ordeal is done, we may just come out of it better.

We adapted to this isolation, we started creating challenges, we were bored but then became curious about things, that now, we had time for. The question is, when lockdown is over, what are we going to do? Will I keep running? Will people still bake?

I started running. It was okay at first but only at first, the first mile was absolute agony, but I read about this. Back when the gyms were open, I was doing five days a week before work on the treadmill, always doing around six kilometres. Monday to Friday, took the weekends off. The Mondays were always so hard because your body had to readjust after the weekend, and I knew when I did those runs on Monday, I was in pain for the first third of It, but after a while your body recognises the routine. It slowly comes back to you and your body essentially shifts a gear and it becomes like walking and that is precisely what happened when I got to the 3.5-mile mark.

I was flying, and I wasn't even breathing heavily. I knew I had to slow my pace down. I had to not get carried away. But I felt like sprinting. I had to remember my head, I had thirteen days of this to go. Straight. No rest. But you just take things one day at a time.

The thing is when you've run fourteen to fifteen days straight already and take a break, it's hard. Yeah, I had some niggles and a little pain, and I was fatigued, but I could do it. I was able to complete the run.

Taking a rest day was the equivalent of me walking the seven miles, or even just stopping for a few seconds to do my shoelace. It has to be hard; you need to be disciplined to set yourself your own rules.

I couldn't stop. If I stopped, then I may have as well just not do it. I never stop for anything during a long-distance race otherwise I think I've cheated. Even during my half-marathons,

I would never stop for a piss, for water, for anything. I just kept jogging.

It's a peculiar metaphor for life; you have to just be consistent and keep moving, never stop for anything. The second you stop, distractions flood inside, excuses invite themselves in and you can't help but allow it. Whatever it is your doing in life, whatever goal you are trying to reach, just don't stop. That is honestly the key to achieving goals, even dreams. This is what my thought process was during my run; however, I'm glad to say I was slightly wrong.

When you come back from two days off, the first run in the bag is the best feeling in the world. I remember on day one, when I got that first seven miles in the bag, it was just magic. I couldn't think about the month ahead, like I didn't think about the week ahead, when I was running on the treadmill, you just take it one day at a time. Get over that preliminary hurdle and you will be flying. Best thing about running is knowing your routine, looking out for those landmarks, those frequent people that are there, at the same time.

The signs and the posters from the Black Lives Matter Campaign were all still up there and the occasional nods to the familiar other joggers who do the same route as you. It was good. It was good to be back.

I knew I had some energy in me, and I knew it was my day off so I did an extra mile and It was still early so I wasn't burning through my day off.

I managed to run exactly eight miles which was the result of my playlist. I just happened to be listening to Eminem when I was around the 6.5-mile mark. It was the track 'Lose Yourself', from the film *8 Mile* and the song itself is like five minutes long. I knew I could run more than half a mile in five minutes so I knew the song would still be going even when I got past seven miles, so I thought, *why the hell not*, I can do another mile without causing any repercussions.

And so, I did. This was a good feeling because now, I knew that I would have to do less distance in the next fourteen days. I mean I would be shaving something like 0.1 miles off, but it makes a difference. Trust me. I think it was realistic to know, I wouldn't be having another day, but what I could do is shave off the distance on my last run on June 30th.

The day flew by when I got back from my run. It felt like doing day one all over again. The energy had worked from the two days off and I managed to run eight miles in one-hour and fifteen minutes.

That took me to 110.7 miles in total. The light at the end of the tunnel was getting brighter.

Despite the days off, my legs were still evidently recovering from the last two week. It was a slow time, I was averaging nine-minute miles, but like Richard said, do not think about the time, just finish the run.

The most important thing, is finishing, forget about your personal time, just get there. I was oblivious enough to say earlier, that I shouldn't stop otherwise I feel like I'm cheating, well when push comes to shove, if in the next two weeks, I stop because my legs can't handle it anymore, I will find a way to finish.

Just got to keep moving. If you want to stop fine, it's okay too but you must figure it out, you must figure how to keep moving.

I'm mentioning this all now, because as predicted, Arsenal lost 3-0 to Man City.

I'm already wishing for football to be cancelled again. It was eerie watching football with no crowds - you did have an option to have the crowd sound on, which was bizarre. It's just normal to us, to have a full crowd when a premiership game is going on.

But, in football it's not over after one game, one heavy defeat - it's about the whole season, it's about finishing in the best possible position. There will be moments, unfortunately like today, where we lost because David Luiz was stupid enough to get sent off, but you learn from it. The important thing is you just don't stop, no matter what. Stopping doesn't mean, you've stopped moving; I was ignorant to say that.

Just like they do in *Cool Runnings* when the sled topples right at the very end. They are all upside down, they are battered, but all four pick themselves up and carry the sled to the finish line. It's so critical not to give up when the odds are against you, just keep moving, keep figuring a way through.

Michael Jordan, one of the best, if not the best, basketball player of all time, said: don't stop if you hit a brick wall, do not turn around and run. Figure a way to break through, or to climb over it, just work your way around it.

It was good to see that football was back, much to Arsenal bloody loosing, it brought people together again in their own homes, a taste of normality returning but we still have a long way to go.

The world stopped, it got hit with something completely unexpected, something no one thought we would see in our lifetimes. We got brought down to our knees. But we got up, we adapted, we worked around this brick wall and now we are moving again, things are starting to look ordinary again. Now we've just got to keep moving. I've got to keep moving.

> 1) It only seems impossible at first but once you attempt it, it turns from impossible to really hard - and the more you keep digging away at something, that thing that was once impossible becomes achievable.
>
> 2) If you do stop, do not let that determine or connote failure. Re-evaluate and figure a way forward. There is always a way forward. It's impossible for there not to be. The worst thing is to not get back up and keep trying.
>
> 3) If I walked the seven miles, I would still be accomplishing my goal. Ego needs to take a backseat here. The key here, is just worry about finishing, don't worry about how, or how long, or what people think, just get there and the rest will fall into place.

17

Setbacks and struggles

The motivation to achieve something is not all plain sailing. The wind will attack you unexpectedly, from any direction and always when you least expect it.

Running is simple from an outside perspective. It's all about moving forward - that's all there is to it. That's life. We've taken a hit right now, a massive hurricane that seems to be lasting an eternity called COVID-19, but what experiences like this tells you, what setbacks or struggles like this pandemic is going to teach, is that we are adaptable, and we need to use these moments to learn from.

More importantly, we can use them to learn more about ourselves and what keeps us moving forward. Arnold Schwarzenegger would always smile when he was at the gym. Michael Jordan would always be out on the court practising, and he would be missing shot after shot. He said he missed more shots than he made. The similarities in their mindset is they have a goal - the misses of the basket or the hours spent at the gym were time they needed to become victorious.

For me, everything that goes wrong is an opportunity to learn something new about yourself, and it's the most valuable lesson - making mistakes, provoking setbacks. You want to embrace them. With that mindset, I have managed to keep moving forward. Something pushes me to the side or pushes me back a little - but my mind will make sure I still move forward.

Remember: driving one straight road is good and all, but what do you learn? Just the path that you already knew, a route you planned for. But being diverted by traffic, by taking new routes, by seeing things you hadn't experienced before - that's where the opportunity presents itself to learn. So how do I comeback from setbacks and struggles? I've learnt to accept that they are key to better improving. That's why Arnold was always smiling at the gym, and that's why Michael Jordan has no shame in saying he missed more shots than he made. Life is all about learning and adapting, just like everyone has with this pandemic.

18

The second day off

And we are back at it. Felt like going back to work after a week's holiday. Okay, no it wasn't that bad, I'm being a tad melodramatic but that day off, was understandably, what I needed.

The danger with having just one day off is you know, in your mind, your back at it tomorrow. It's why Saturdays or the first three or four days of your week holiday are the best and then, when it gets to Sunday or the last couple of days of your holiday, you start thinking about going back, even though you're off, you're away, you're on holiday but you're mind, of course, is looking ahead, calculating.

Got to check my emails, got to unpack, have to get my lunches ready for work and suddenly your time off, your holiday, has been contaminated with deliberations of work.

With only having one day off, you don't really have time to accommodate the idea of imminent thoughts, however they do crop up now and again, you just have to keep focused on enjoying your day off, slightly contradictory, I know, but it's what you need to do.

My alarm had been set for six in the morning. Your mind, as amazing as it is, does have the ability to piss you off. The second you programme something in there, like knowing you must get up for six for the next day, it will do the complete opposite.

Yesterday, I was up like a bird at 6.30 because my mind knew I didn't have to be up until 7.30. Why is that? Well, I could get all the scientific reasoning about it but it really comes down to your state of mind.

It's just simply your feelings towards the day ahead. Subconsciously, I'm not looking forward to going to work, so my internal watch is not in a rush to get up, hence why I missed that alarm that one day.

Weekends, or days off, or holiday, my body is relaxed and I'm happy and therefore, my body will wake me up because I'm in a positive mind set. Like I said: it's all about that sodding mind set.

It was now 6.15. I had finished all my press-ups and I was ready to go for my run and then I came to the realisation that my headphones wouldn't charge in time.

It was then, that I decided to go back to bed and wait ten minutes. What a mistake that was. I mean could run without them but an hour with no music or the sound of a film, nothing, just your thoughts, was something that I hadn't done yet. I mean I had, but not throughout this challenge.

You do however, see those top athletes running marathon and they don't listen to music. It's mainly because when doing an actual event, you need to be able to listen to sirens or important changes. That's what I was told when I wanted to listen to my music during a running event, so I assume that's why. I knew what I was doing deep down, I was trying to talk myself out of it.

You know when you look back at something and wish you didn't do one thing - well that was my one thing, going back to bed.

I remember figuring out the calculations of my remaining runs. All that time yesterday at work, doing the maths in my head, figuring out different ways I could schedule my remaining runs.

I could have another day off if I carried on doing seven miles like I did for the first fifteen days. My subconscious had taken over. I stayed in bed and I just couldn't get out of bed. By then, Fran had snuggled up to me.

This was the problem. I had a choice, I could afford to do it, and that left me vulnerable. I didn't go running that day; I stayed in bed and despite not even falling back asleep, I was still well rested.

This now meant I would now have to run from tomorrow to the end of the month without a rest day, no matter what.

This eliminated the option of choice and meant that I had no excuse under the sun to miss any runs now.

I had applied the pressure back on myself like I did when I made sure everyone knew about this challenge, so I had no choice but to do it. Applying pressure forces you to come out of your shell otherwise what are you going to find out about yourself if you stay in your comfort zone.

I had realised this during my second week of running that I wouldn't be doing this challenge, if I hadn't applied this self-inflicting pressure on myself. It had to be done this way otherwise your mind will convince yourself you have an option to go the other way and today I learnt that.

By doing the calculations yesterday I had programmed into my head that I had an alternative. That I had, another day off if I carried on doing the same thing and that was probably not a good move but at the same time, I learnt something.

The only reason I am doing this is because I told everyone I was doing it, I signed up for a charity, I raised money, and I told everyone about it. There was really no turning back from this. And before this started, it felt amazing realising I had been stripped of choice here, that I must do this.

I gave myself no choice. Remember when I said, the longer you think about doing something, the longer you allow yourself to talk yourself out of it, well this is what I did here. I took action with this challenge to make sure I couldn't do that. I gave myself no plan B. It was either do it or don't do and if I didn't do it, everyone would know. I applied that pressure on myself and to a degree; I think that's what I subconsciously done here again. It was dangerous taking two days off back-to-back. I was now going to get use to this rest day, more importantly, two days of not running.

What's done is done now, I need to quickly stop dwelling and accept that I've made this decision and look to the bright side, which is, I have another day to rest my body. Maybe it is for the best, I mean, I did just run fourteen days straight so I can do it again and now with two days' rest, I'll be fresher, that's the logic.

But I realised come tomorrow, I will have no choice but to run and continue it for the next fourteen days. The problem this time is I don't have the safety net of taking a day off. Screw logic, this was reckless, I don't have a single reason to stop, otherwise that's game over, or I have to run fourteen miles in one day, which I just can't picture doing.

There was no turning away from this now; I had used my last lifeline because my headphones were not working. Truthfully, I could have run without music but it wouldn't have been fun, but if I'm being honest with myself, it was just an excuse that I let in. That's all it took to change the course of today, and consequently, the next fourteen days. Just like when that alarm didn't go off and just like today, because I didn't charge my headphones, it takes the smallest of cracks in your routine for the whole thing to come crashing down.

Yesterday when I was having my rest day, I figured out that I could have another rest day, which meant my mind knew I had a safety net and it just needed a sign somewhere, to just take over my initial decision of running today. Safety nets are bollocks.

This was all going through my head that morning in bed when I should have been running outside. It's always annoying when it got to half-seven. I could have run seven miles by now and I would then, only have to run 6.5 miles from then on with a break whenever I needed it. That looks more attractive now than it ever has done. Is this break worth it? It certainty did not feel like it right now.

Our conversations were being drained by the sound of the TV in the background. The usually, COVID updates, news and fatalities across the world kept coming up and forcing me to turn my head towards the TV. It didn't really distract me; it was common background noise now, the updates of the world and the handling of this pandemic. Hell, I swear I heard Boris

Johnson's voice more than my girlfriend.

Another big piece of news was the football was returning tomorrow, more specifically Arsenal returning tomorrow. They were playing Man City, god help us. I totally forgot the football was back on. It bought a little smile to me but It wasn't enough to convince Fran that it was genuine. She could tell. She always can.

Fran knew, that if the sound of football couldn't distract me, then I must have been serious about what I was talking about. She knew I was having this mental struggle with taking this second day off. I piled on the pressure.

Fran knew I had come to a realisation. Offer yourself no choice or excuses and you will have to push forward, maybe that's why I did it.

Let's hope I can put this into practise. No days off now. This is the second half of the stretch now and I just made it mentally harder. No days off. There was no safety net. Another steppingstone into discovering more about what makes you push forward.

1) Having a safety net doesn't allow you to fully commit. We perform one hundred percent better if we don't have a safety net, a backup. Eliminating the safety will bring you to a harsh realisation; you have no choice but to commit.

2) Do not contaminate your days off with thoughts of work or working. Doing this wastes your present state of resting.

3) The smallest of things can change the whole course of your day. You already know this probably but when it does happen, do not entertain that thing as an excuse not to continue with your planned day.

19

Four days to go

You guessed it. My weekend off and I still got up early. Okay, not early, but around 7.30ish - so a ninety-minute improvement on the days where I have to work. I had the strangest yet most satisfying feeling inside of me, I was so comfortable in bed right now, so content. Just in bed with Fran next to me, relaxing, with four days to go.

I could hear the wind whistling which is just the cherry on top of my current state right now. All I need now is a fireplace and for it to start snowing outside. The hot weather had its moment and I fought it head on, running seven-mile runs during that ordeal, three whole days of it.

When you look back at something that you once were dreading, you realise how it wasn't as bad as you made it out to be. You just have to be organised with it. I ran in the mornings when it was cool, and I did everything I could to avoid the intense heat. This is why planning is important; you can prepare and more importantly, you can plan your day.

I checked my brand-new Apple watch and on the main screen it shows me the hourly forecast for the weather. This would have been handy earlier on this month. It indicated that at nine, an hour or so from now, we would be expecting rain. I tried to ignore it, but my eyes had already seen it. Kind of impossible to ignore that information now. As content as I was, I had some energy in me, I felt loosened, I was recharged, I just felt great. At first, I thought it was just lying-in bed in a comfortable spot with the sound of the wind, but it was more than that. I was a hundred percent recharged and I have no idea why, maybe it was the extra ninety-minute lie in, maybe that's all it takes.

It was around eight-ish that I got up and I did my press ups and by then, I was wide awake. Didn't feel fatigued, I didn't feel the need to stretch my legs or pity myself, it was like walking around on the first day of this challenge, fresh. I even smashed through the press ups without even procrastinating. Fran had woken up and blamed me, even though I was very careful in not waking her up when I got out of bed.

She told me to get back to bed and without any hesitation, I did. I didn't have a single negative thought in my body, I couldn't say no to anything, I was floating in the air. Perhaps because it was Saturday, but I know days don't define me, so what's going on? I was absolutely buzzing. I should never challenge a positive feeling, just go with it.

We spend our lives worrying all the time because we are a species that just can't help it, we even worry about the good things happening to us, we become cautious and when we do that, we don't enjoy the moment.

We had been watching *SAS: Who Dares Win*, and we've been enjoying it so far; the tasks and exercise these lads had to do were both excruciating and fascinating. I was watching it the whole time thinking I could probably do something like this.

It's very easy to say it sitting pretty on a sofa. It's like watching gameshows and getting annoyed with the contestant because they don't know the answer, or a footballer for not scoring and saying you could have scored that. We have the luxury of having no pressure, pressure is everything. Can you imagine performing in front of a live audience or playing football in a packed Wembley arena. Suddenly those questions you know, become frizzled, those football skills you have become rusty, it's all about keeping your mind in the game, keeping your eye on the prize.

On SAS, they had these challenge where the aim of the tasks was to eliminate three other people by lasting as long as you can on this task called 'The Sickener'. It would be excruciating drills like running up and down horrible terrains, press ups and with a forty-pound bag on, it was just brutal. And they would keep going until someone takes off their armband off, which means they give up, they can't take anymore.

One guy was still running but his legs were gone, he was just grinding through, just so determined to pull through, no matter what. All this was crossing my mind as I was just lying there in bed.

Fran rose up from her sleeping position and started reading *The Fear Bubble*, another book by Anthony Middleton. Funny, she picked that book up just as I was reminiscing over the show from yesterday.

This burst of energy was in me. I knew that I wanted to smash below an hour for a seven miler but didn't want to do it near the beginning in case it fatigued me or worse, got an injury. I had planned to do it on the last day but in my head,

I was thinking, *fuck it,* let's give it a go. The thing is, I didn't know I was going to do I until I started running. I mean it was in my mind but when you start running you just try and get into a comfortable routine during a challenge.

I was told to take it easy, don't worry about time and be smart.

I had four runs to go and one of them was today and if I did seven miles for three of those runs, I would only have to do 4.3 miles for the 30th. So, if I did run fast and die inside and worse yet, cause an injury, I had the safety in knowing, all I really need to do is 4.3 miles.

Fran ended up in the spare room reading and I walked by and told her to wait for me for breakfast. It had reached 8.20. The skies were getting dark. I need to get ahead of this weather before it chucks it down. Days ago, I was worrying about the heat, now the opposite.

Just as I was walking away, Fran popped her head up and said: 'I'll wait for you for breakfast, will you be long?'

'No, I won't, I'll be back in an hour.'

For some reason, that gave me another little boost and I was feeling good. I burst out the door, sorted out my playlist and off I went. I noticed my pace was quicker but there was no way I could keep this going surely. As I got past Cemetery Junction, it fucking started spraying with rain. Like if you felt the debris of the wind blowing a sprinkler towards you. It wasn't even nine yet.

Fucking weather app. Can never trust it. However, by the time I reached Palmer Park, I couldn't feel any precipitation. I wasn't sure if it was because of how light the rain was or the covering of the trees, but it was nice and dry and more importantly, not hot.

My pace was surprisingly good. I must have been doing eight-minute miles or less. My strides were a lot longer and more common and I was smashing the first lap.

In my head I knew I would have to slow down by the second lap. Remember I must do five laps of this park before returning back home on the long stretch on London Road.

By lap two, my pace was still going strong. There were times when I would slow down but I shouted at myself and continued the pace. I used people running in front of me as targets to overtake. I imagined I was racing them, and I had to beat them to that landmark up ahead. It was clear, my head was in in a very good mindset this morning.

By lap three I was still maintaining this speed. I didn't want to check my phone to see how far I'd done on my relive app, or what the time was, I just wanted to hold this pace. Every now and again my mind would talk me out of this pace, but a stronger voice would tell me to just keep running. I wasn't sprinting but I wasn't jogging either. Nothing about what I was doing signified I had been running for fifty days before this, clocking in over two-hundred and fifty miles.

I always found when I was doing Half-marathons that the hardest mile is always the last one. Even though in your head you've been waiting to see mile thirteen to appear on those little boards.

Mile thirteen is the hardest not because your body has just run twelve miles but because you know you're almost finished, so your body relaxes and gets ready to shut down, to stop. That is the same in any distance you do, if you're doing a three-mile run or a twenty six-mile run. The last mile or the last kilometre are always the hardest which is why I try never to look at the clock when I'm on a treadmill because I know I'm only running thirty minutes. Think it was Bill Gates who said, *'Look at the clock when you are sitting idle, but never look at the clock when you're working.'*

If I saw the clock on the treadmill back when I was doing those runs at the gym and it read twenty-seven minutes, I knew those three minutes will be the longest three minutes of my life. The best part of running is the limbo stage and that's the second to fourth lap of the park for me. Just in free fall with your pace. You're just comfortable and nothing will stop you and the pain of running isn't flooding your mind.

As I departed Palmer Park and onto London Road, it was really kicking in, the feelings of pain, the feeling that I had to stop. I had to maintain the pace. I was thinking about this moment on lap one, which seemed a lifetime away. I was starting to figure out that even with this pace, I probably would only beat an hour by a matter of seconds, hopefully more but that's the sort of margins we are talking about here.

The difference between the one hundred-metre record from 1912 to today's record is simply just a tad over a second. 1.02 second to be exact. 1.02 development from Donald Lippincott's record of 10.6 in 1912 to Usain Bolts record of 9.58 in 2009. Although technically, four Germans had run 10.5 in the qualifiers in 1912 and Donald was even beaten by his teammates when he ran the 10.6 but it was his name that was on the record books for some reason.

I might not have even beaten an hour, but I've definitely given it a go. Usually, I frown upon that sort of submissive brushing off response to a challenge. I always hated people going, 'I gave it my best shot' or 'I've enjoyed myself'.

You don't want to be happy or sugarcoat that failure with a cop-out response like that, you need to be upset and annoyed and move on. If you did your best, then you need to go again. I knew I could do this; I've done it before, well maybe not after running for fifty days but my body and my mind were right, I knew I could do this, I shouldn't entertain the possibility of failing already. I'm still in the moment.

My legs were now starting to ache as I got to the home stretch and I could feel myself wanting to slow down but I was grinding though. I could throw all this hard work away by my mind getting the better of me on this 0.6 mile stretch to the finish, the hardest part mentally. I wanted to look at my phone, but I didn't. I stayed composed and carried on the pace, it was slower, but I was maintaining it. Now usually, with no prior running and proper training, I could smash out seven miles in probably less than fifty-five minutes, maybe less than that, so I was expecting the time to be under an hour but I just didn't know how quick or slow I was going.

I just told myself, it must be less than an hour. I know I've gone fast today and luckily with no repercussions afterwards. Well, we will find out when I stop. When you stop after a long run, never just stop, always gradually slow down into a walk- and carry-on walking for at least another minute. Trust me, that's how you will get an injury. Very common way.

I ran past Cemetery Junction and saw the last stretch. I

sprinted. As I sprinted, I got ready to stop my relive app which meant I would see what time I did.

I saw it! I did seven miles, and I was still running. The clock was reading fifty-eight minutes and forty-three seconds. Oh my god. There you go! I felt great. I slowed down and broke into a walk with the biggest smile on my face. And the greatest thing about it, my breathing was fine, and my legs were in good nick. I could probably keep going. The fitness was coming back at a higher level. With three days to go, I was wondering, am I really going to stop this newfound achievement. I needed time to compose myself, let's not my emotion carry me away here. I knew I could do it and I did it.

When I got back, I told Fran everything, every little detail. My good mood continued as a result and it carried for the rest of the day. It's amazing how positive energy spreads, one smile will make someone else smile. Start your day strong and the rest will fall into place. I saw my parents later that day so we could celebrate my dad's birthday a few days ago. I told them about today's run, but they didn't care nearly as much as I did, and that was okay, I was on cloud nine.

I managed to run one of the days in less than an hour and I've got three runs to go and only two of them are seven-mile runs. Today was a great day and as we were coming to the end of this challenge, I had started to appreciate the journey I've been on and also, the journey that I will be on after this ends in three days' time.

1) You have no idea what you're capable of until you try it. A lot of people think they can't do something and sometimes they are right, but to attempt the impossible takes courage and you could fail and you probably will, but then you do it again and again and again. And today, it took me twenty-seven days to get there. I don't know how, it just happened because I kept strong, I kept determined and I reached a mindset that I did not have in those previous twenty-six days. One of the greatest tragedies in life is peoples unfulfilled potential.

2) Don't think about failing when it hasn't happened yet. I started doubting myself during one of my runs a long time ago and I was already giving myself excuses, 'I did my best' and all those rubbish cop-outs. It's not over until it's over. Dig deep and never submit until it's finish. That very mindset is the reason people fail because it gets hard, it gets tough and you submit to it. See it through and fight it all the way until the end, believe you can last the entire run, or project or challenge. Until the end.

3) It doesn't matter how little you've progressed, the important thing is, that you have. Only a second separates the world record for the one-hundred metre from 1912 until today and imagine all the work and sweat that went into achieving that one second gap. Progress means moving forward at any rate. Celebrate any achievement you can.

20
Triumph and reflection

The most important thing about living your life is doing something you didn't believe you could do. In that journey, if you have the will to keep going, to keep putting a foot in front of another, you have no idea the self-discovery you start to unlock.

There's a lot of poetic bullshit I could say about achieving your goal or doing something you thought you couldn't do, or that someone else thought you couldn't do. But it comes down to breaking your norm. It comes down to determination and grinding, fighting off laziness, normal routine or even tiredness. The easy option is always going to be there, and that is to give up because things get harder as you progress. But it doesn't matter when you get there it just matters that you do get there eventually.

Too many people don't know what they want to do in life, just bouncing off ideas every now and again and then doing something else later. Those people are lost. Having an aim, having a goal, is everything. It will fuel your mentality to be stronger; it will unlock doors for you in life. Achieving something great is only great because you achieved it through the thick and thin. It was only achievable because you kept moving forward. Sometimes, you will latch on to an excuse - too tired, too lazy, can't be bothered - and that will happen; but remember, deep down, you can always find another level. You just to dig deep.

As Muhammed Ali said: suffer now and live the rest as a champion.

21

Nearly there

There comes a time when we must relish the moment; you must recognise that you've done well and just stay in that moment for as long as you can. Yesterday, I did my challenge within a challenge; I ran seven miles under an hour, with fifty days' worth of running in my body. It's amazing what the body can do but what it really comes down to is how you programme your train of thought to confronting these tasks. Thinking you can do something is half of the obstacle gone, the rest is doing it.

Some people think tasks can't be achieved because they seem unreachable at first glance, but I tell you something, step on the ladder and climb it and find out how far you can go, and you might just surprise yourself. I certainly did. Logic aside, my legs should be in agony, I should have some repercussions, I shouldn't really be able to smash out a run that quickly.

It wouldn't be that quick for some runners, especially elite runners or ultra-runners, but I'm a normal guy who just likes running, and I surprised myself today. What else can I surprise myself with? One of the greatest things you can do is surprise yourself. Once you've done it once, you may just have the bug.

I had nothing else to prove, I was so close to the finish line, I was feeling relaxed. That feeling of victory was there. I began to look back at all the obstacles I had gone through to get where I am now. I started to realise that running below an hour was great, but I knew others had done better, I knew some of my friends could do better. Yes of course, I ran fifty days prior to that but still; you can't help but question your achievements when you get there. At first glance it's meant to be impossible and yet when you get there, you soak in the victory and then something weird happens, you question if it was in fact worth the stress and worry and build up, because believe or not, it wasn't impossible, it was achievable, by someone who's not a great runner.

It was a weird moment and that's why I always tell people to celebrate their victories, don't dumb it down, you took that step on the ladder and you climbed and you got there. I must, however, stay focused because it's not quite over yet.

Now that I've run under an hour throughout my two-hundred miles, I had nothing more to prove. My fastest run before yesterday was day three, when I clocked in around sixty-one minutes. Took me twenty-five days to beat that time by a whole three minutes. Now that's progress. Progress is baby steps, it's making mistakes, breaking obstacles, progress, is never going backwards.

Just look all the moving parts that got Apollo 11 to the moon.

The Russians provoked them. They were the first to send a satellite into orbit, Sputnik. The first satellite put into orbit and thus started this space race. Without this friendly competition, we might not have gone to the moon. They failed and failed and failed over and over again, before they successfully landed on the moon in 1969. Even with Yuri Gagarin becoming the first men in space, the Americans still refused to stop trying, they still kept going. They failed down here so they could succeed up there. People died, tests went wrong, they were exploring unfamiliar territory, but they did it and seven more Apollo missions followed. It's not impossible until it done but it's only possible if you don't give up, if you don't turn around and fall at the first hurdle. The Russians beat them with Sputnik, first satellite in space, then the first man in orbit but no, they kept pushing forward and because they did, sacrifices aside, they achieved greatness, '*One small step for men.*'

And that is progress, it's just small steps, that's all progress is. So, don't fret if you don't think you're not going anywhere, you are. Rome was not built in a day. When you start to get nearer to the end of this so-called impossible task, when you finally realised, that what you're doing, what you've been working towards, isn't impossible, you start to grow a perspective that you've never had before, a perspective you've earned that will stay with you for the rest of your life, on how to tackle obstacles, on how to see things through, on how to not give up. But first things first. Let's complete today's run. We're almost there.

In my head I knew all I had to do was run seven miles today, tomorrow and then 4.3 miles on Tuesday. I couldn't believe how far I've come. When I ran that first seven miles on June 1st, I couldn't believe for a second that I could carry it on, but I knew that I wouldn't stop no matter what. Worst case scenario if I did get injured or just mentally battered, I would walk the entire thing, but god knows how long that would take me. I feel like I'm two sets up in a tennis match with a break in the third set or, 3-0 up at halftime in football. As certain as things may look, anything can happen, and they tend to happen at the worst moment. This challenge has definitely been evident of that. Yes, I'm close but I'm not finished yet. I still need to cross that finish line; I still need to step off that zip wire.

Once again, I woke up quite early, and it was perfect conditions for the run. Fran was still asleep. I kid you not, nothing is better than going for a run on a day off, really early in the morning, getting back and showered and returning back to bed with your girlfriend still in bed. Going back to bed next to her warm body after eating your frog for the day was an amazing feeling. The day was completely yours. It's one of the best feelings ever.

I tried to do that yesterday, but she was already up. Today, I snuck past her and went out the back and did it quietly as possible. I used the thought of getting back to bed as extra fuel for today's run. It was just before nine when I set off. Fran was out cold when I left, and I hope she will be when I get back so I can return to bed with her. We were up late last night so fingers cross.

In my head, once this run was in the bag, I knew the next day would be my last seven-miler. It was a somewhat emotional but at the same time I was relived. I had raised over three-hundred and fifty pounds for East African Playgrounds, which was two-hundred and fifty pounds above target so I was pleased with that. They emailed me congratulating me again and asked me to do a blog and a video on why I chose them. It wasn't that hard. If I can make any kids lives better, I will do it. I would always get angry if I saw people suffer and now, I'm an adult and can take real steps in making a change in my own way. This challenge probably won't be the end, but this is a wakeup call on what I can do. I won't be doing it, but it challenged myself to think three-hundred miles next month, which is like ten miles a day, I would find a way to do it and the funny thing is, I know it's possible now. The impossible are not impossible to me anymore. I've gained; I've earned a perspective to see things like that now. That is what this whole challenge was about, believing that these things are possible, above speculation.

It's another three miles on top of what I did, every day. I don't want to entertain this notion otherwise I will get to a point of no turning back on the idea. Is that a bad thing though?

My breathing was similar to if I was walking. It got to that point now where I had finally found myself in running; I had found that freedom to it. I read what other runners talked about, this feeling of gliding and not fighting against the current; it makes sense now and it's a great feeling.

You put yourself through eighty percent of pain so you can get that twenty percent pleasure, and that twenty percent pleasure is only pleasurable if you grind through that eighty. This formula works for most things, working Monday to Friday and the weekend being the pleasurable part. And the harder you grind through that eighty percent, the more satisfactory that twenty percent becomes. In essence, the more you work hard, you more liberating the glory becomes.

Running seven miles so I can be in bed with my girlfriend. That was my only thought process. Of course, for the whole day after the run you feel amazing, you feel like this day wasn't wasted, and that's how you want to feel. You want to put the time in so you can enjoy yourself afterwards and in peace. Sometimes talking yourselves out of things happen all the time and you will never ever realise your full potential.

My greatest fear, it's not spiders, it's not snakes; it's unfilled potential. And the more you discover it, you more you want to explore it. It's about the journey, and my journey is coming to an end.

I finished my seven miles jog and I started walking back to my flat. I was surprised to see that my time was just short of sixty-four minutes, one of my fastest runs. Proof right there that this is truly mind over body, and that gave me great encouragement to really utilise my way of thinking. I can programme my mind to enhance what I can do with my body, anyone can, and this notion felt incredible, that I had power over this.

I had 11.6 miles left. That's all it was. I'm basically there.

I quietly opened the backdoor, after my run, and yes, she was still asleep. That's great news. The only reason she would wake up now is to go to the toilet and I'm about to go in there and shower so I know she will stay in bed, warming up the bed. I'm telling you, the second I got out the shower and I laid down next to her and she put her head on my chest, I can tell you this: for that I would run seven miles. I would run twenty miles a day just for this.

That twenty percent is something you need to earn. I earned it. The truth is, that twenty percent can last the entire day, the entire week if you want it to, so make sure you deserve it, work hard for it. 80/20. Earn your twenty. When I said you could apply it to anything, you really can. This lockdown is honestly the grind the world is going through right now: the NHS, the government, and the people who are losing work, people who have mental illness. It's getting crazy and we don't know when things will get back to normal. Not knowing something, not knowing what is going to happen is a scary notion but with each day, we take baby steps. We solve one problem at a time, we grind through the hard work, like the Apollo mission, like me on day one and the world has had tremendous obstacles; but we have not turned around, we have carried on pushing forward and the day is coming where this lockdown will be over, where we will have a vaccine and when we reach that point of pleasure, that twenty percent, that light at the end of this very long and unknown tunnel.

1) Victory, glory, accomplishments taste greater when you've worked towards them. The harder you work, the sweeter the victory, the greater the glory. Don't look for short cuts, if you find them then you simply be strong and block it, deflect it and continue on your path.

2) Progress is 'small steps' remember. Do not rush your progress, do not look back and start creating doubt. The important thing is, is that you keep moving forward.

3) Perspective is everything. How you see the world, how you see people, how you don't judge certain people is what makes you who you are. How you view a task is your attitude towards either tackling it or giving up at the first hurdle. Work on your perspective; be open with the thought that with hard work, the impossible can be chiselled into something possible.

22

Time

A long time ago, someone decided that the norm would be five days a week where we work, and off for two on the weekends. Weekends, I think we can agree, are just not long enough. It's two days. And on the second day, the Sunday, we start to dwell about going to work on the Monday, so you consume some of your weekend worrying about the next five days. This somewhat gets counter acted on Friday when we finish work, and we get ready for the weekend. Most get that 'Friday Feeling' where we get this buzz and freedom that we can kick back and just relax or make plans before Monday comes peeking around the corner again.

The point is it doesn't matter what day it is, it's all about how you use the time that is available to you, and how you feel towards doing it. Today being Monday has no impact on me whatsoever. Monday shouldn't define my day, just like being a Virgo shouldn't define who I am.

I've managed to run the last fifty odd days with time I have created for myself. Some days I have less time to play around with, but the time is there. You simply just need to organise it. I keep mentioning the word, perspective. Now that I'm coming to the end of this journey, I've realised that when this ends, I will have more time back.

The twenty minutes in the mornings for me to get in the right mind set, where I brush my teeth, do my press ups and get my gear on. The run, the max it took me to run seven miles during this challenge was day fourteen, the day before my unexpected two days off. It took me sixty-eight minutes to run that day.

Fourteen is my lucky number but like I said, nothing vague should define you. I can't expect things to fall on the fourteenth to magically line up for me simply because I like a certain number. In fact, it makes me happy I had the longest run on that day because it shows that nothing like numbers or star signs, or days of the week or certain holidays, have any reflection on certain moods.

You don't have to rest on Sundays, you don't need to be grumpy on Mondays, you don't need to be cautious on Friday the 13th. We need to own it; we need to break this lazy way of thinking, of putting things into vague categories and just power through. They slow us down and this challenge has shown me how far you can really go if you just organise your time, and that's the important component with anything, your time, and what you do with it.

So, that's twenty minutes plus my maximum running time, which is sixty-eight minutes. Then my cool down which consists of editing my Relive Video, uploading my video, and sticking it on Instagram whilst choosing a track of the day, that's around fifteen minutes. That's one-hundred and three minutes I've found everyday throughout the last month so

I could do this challenge. I would say I've carved that time out, but truth be told, I've been wasting time doing random rubbish at the start of lockdown, playing the X-Box, watching random films that I've seen before. After my run tomorrow, I will have one-hundred and three minutes available to me. How will I substitute that time? What will I do? Lockdown has horrible and unprecedented as it is, has opened my eyes, and has forced some people to adapt to something no one expected: more time.

However, you can create your own weekends; you can choose to have your Mondays off and work the Saturday or work over Christmas and get your triple pay - it's just another day after all. Today was just another day, another day where I have to run seven miles, but today was significant. It was the last day that I would run seven miles.

Back in May, my big runs were five miles, and I was dreading that. I've reached a point now where anything less than seven miles puts a smile on my face - who would of thought that when I was attempting to run five kilometres in April and struggling to breathe. How much two months have changed me. Making anything your norm offers perspective for things you once thought were hard. The advantage of a challenge, if you stay consistent, is that anything less becomes the norm to you. If the norm for you is now running ten miles a day, then five miles is a walk in the park.

Come July 4th, the restrictions were going to be dropped from two metres to one metre distancing, and restaurant and cinemas – and, more importantly, pubs - would reopen. The date was rather fitting, don't you think? Independence Day.

That would mark the official end of this lockdown. And these past three and half months will soon be a distant memory, an anecdote for our children - what did you do during it? How did it affect you? What did you do with the luxury of time?

It wasn't as positive as I made it out to be. I mean, we weren't taken to shelters underground with the sounds or air raids every now and again, if anything, we were quite fortunate because all we had to do was sit tight. Given history, this wasn't hard to fight; however, has history does prove, this species is not particularly good at following the rules. It got to a point during the three and a half months where the new norm had dissolve; not many people carried on with their newfound enjoyment of this situation. The baking had stop, the quizzes had slowly disappeared, the newfound energy to go running and influence others had stop. It turns out it was a just early fad throughout lockdown. Come July, what will happen to us - will the spikes go back up, will we enter another national lockdown? Only time will tell. The best thing to do with events happening in the world is to keep your head down and focus on yourself. This lockdown acted as one big run and the end was coming now, we had a date, a rather convenient date and that, if you will, signifies the end of lockdown, the end of the run. All you can do is tackle it one day at a time. It's the same attitude I have with my run, one minute at a time, one day at a time.

Well, like the last twenty-nine days - or rather fifty-four days including my hundred-mile challenge in May - I woke up at six and I got ready to do my seven-mile run. But today was special; it was my last seven-mile run. None of that really made it special inside my head, I was still dreading going and

I wanted to stay in bed, but once I got out there, I knew it would be okay. Everything will be okay - that's what you need to keep telling yourself.

The weather was perfect. It was moments away from raining which was beautiful; you know when the sky is talking to you. The wind was the strongest it had been since the whole of June, acting like an effect for my dramatic finish to this challenge, sweeping my hair in a heroic fashion.

The run started becoming effortless. Where was this before? By lap two of Palmer Park, there was nothing to my breathing. I could have stopped and been able to teach an hour seminar on the history of films in the 1970s without breaking a sweat. After twenty-nine days, I started seeing some real changes and the amazing thing is, if you can stay consistent, you will slowly see these changes implement in your life. I was reading more; I was thinking more. I had an awareness of life bigger than I did fifty-four days ago.

This lockdown, as awful as it was, was a real eye opener to many people. If you strip a person of their possessions and social lifestyle, what is left of them? The question was, the question I kept asking myself, what happens when lockdown is over?

During the run today, I thought about stopping. There was always a point on every run where I wanted to stop. I knew I had done 188.6 miles without stopping, so why was I thinking of stopping now? Maybe because it's near the end and I knew I could make up the miles tomorrow. This is the danger when you have a safety net - you start to drag; you start to ease up because you know you're going to be okay if you fail.

Would the tightrope performer be better with or without the safety net; would he be more careful with it there or without it there? A safety net, as attractive as it is, is a distraction, an indication that if you fail, you will be fine. The mind set works better with no back up plan.

I removed my safety rope, when I told everyone I was doing this challenge, so I couldn't back out.

All I had to really do today was 5.6 miles today and tomorrow and I would have reached two-hundred miles. Hell, I could have done 3.8 mile and I would have been fine, just meant running seven tomorrow. But I've already decided I wanted to carry on as normal and have this sprint finish tomorrow, and Fran has already agreed to join me. Plus, both my work and my charity had asked for a photo when I cross that two-hundred-mile mark, so I needed Fran there, and like hell would she be running seven miles with me tomorrow.

The sad thing is when I got onto London Road on the 6.2-mile mark, I felt sad because my routine was coming to an end. This was my last seven-mile run.

When is enough, enough? When should someone stop? What am I proving to people? What am I proving to myself? Suddenly my run and my mental battle with myself stopping turned into a philosophical rant in my head. What more can I do? Is there more? I remember running those one-hundred and ninety-six days at the gym, the challenge that turned into an obsession.

The thing you must remember when running is that once you break routine, things either go sideways or they go downhill. Keep your structure and implement a new routine. Maybe

I'll go back to running four miles five days a week. That was the plan in my head, but I wasn't going to force it. Not like I did for this challenge.

I guess you always want more. And I'm glad I was having this battle with myself. I was growing as a person.

When I ran past my flat and to the sign to make up those extra 0.3 miles, I completed my seven miles and for the first time, I stopped - not slowing down to a walk, but I stopped. I simply just looked up and thought: how have I got this far? What is going to be my next journey? What will I do with this new learned perspective?

I started walking towards the flat, uploaded my video, edited my video, posted my video and then just took two minutes to look around outside.

195.7 miles left to go. Today's run took me sixty-five minutes, which wasn't bad after fifty odd days of running. It was within touching distance now. I just need to run 4.3 miles tomorrow and that was it.

Something in me was hidden but I think I may just have found it now. I found an opportunity to keep going maybe. I didn't want this to end, this had become part of my lifestyle like going to football on Mondays or watching Match of the Day at half ten on Saturdays.

The world was slowing coming back to normal. We even booked a flight to Naples for the end of August. Was I honestly missing lockdown? Did I discover myself during these three and half months? Why did lockdown trigger this mind set?

The key to a great story, a good narrative is making sure that the end of the story, the end of the film or book, is the start of another journey. I don't like endings that just end, as odd as that sounds. A good film ends with the beginning of another story. I believe challenges and tasks are exactly that. When you finish them, then the real journey begins, on how you live your life with this newfound perspective earned from doing this challenge. What did I learn and how will I use it? What did we learn during lockdown? What will come of us when this is over? Come July 4th, Independence Day, our journey, as a nation will begin again.

1) Time is the most important thing in your life; never forget how important it is. Organising your day, owning your decisions is key to achieving your goals. The goals will only happen if you know what time you have on your hands, your knowledge of time in your life is everything because it will determine where you are going, what path you will lead down. If you choose to spend your time eating junk food, then guess where your life is heading. And remember; don't let vague things determine your time. It doesn't say anywhere you can't work on a Saturday or you need to stress on the Monday. The time is yours. You dictate when.

2) Just because something ends doesn't mean that's the end of it, in fact it should mean the complete opposite, it's the start of something new. People diet all the time and then they end their three-month programme and most never stay consistent, never take away what they learnt in those three months. There is a reason you did it, do not let these things becomes a fad, a past time. Learn from it; make it adapt you later in life, to shape you. These are the reasons why we do these things. We have come into a world now where people do things on a dare, or a whim but never try to understand the reasons behind maybe running a marathon or a diet. Make sure you carry on the drive even after it ends. Lockdown will end and it may even come back but make sure you've learnt from last time and utilities that mind set on your life and other upcoming obstacles.

3) Don't entertain quitting just because there may not be any repercussions to you. The seductiveness of a backup or a safety net is predominately the reasons why people go half ass on tasks, challenges or just life. Pushing yourself really takes guts and determination when you know you don't have to. Drop the net and make that climb without the rope and see what happens.

23

Victory

I woke up knowing I only had to do 4.4 miles and that was it, the challenge I had worked so hard to reach, was ultimately coming to an end. It was almost dreamlike that the day had arrived, but it didn't make the day any more distinctive, just moments of gratitude that I had finally made it to this day. It was almost like the lead up to Christmas. The hype, the energy, the build-up to the 25th. You have your initial burst of energy on Christmas morning, and you do everything you can on the day to make it special, the presents, the dinner, the games, seeing families you would never see, and just like any other day, it goes away.

Christmas could fall on a Monday or a Saturday and the day wouldn't define your mood, Christmas itself would trump it. Today, it didn't matter what day it was, what I was going to do, I just knew today, the moment was here that I would complete two-hundred miles in one month, something I thought I honestly, I couldn't do.

When I woke up, all I thought about was how I managed to complete this challenge. It occurred to me that the only reason I got to the end of this challenge, in a nutshell, was because I wasn't being lazy. It's remarkable how many things we don't do because we're lazy. And being lazy defines your characteristics; your attitude towards life, doing things quickly rather than properly, it really changes your approach to things like this, a task, a goal, and a challenge.

As I approach this last chapter, I know some will think this task was possible or some may think it was easy, it was doable. Others may look at this and think this was impossible but here's the important thing: it was impossible to me.

Not because I knew I couldn't physically do it, but because it was doing it with everything that was going on in the world.

The truth be told; I didn't actually have the gift of time. There were some days where I did work from home, but I work in an essential place so therefore I was going into the office, so what spurred me on.

This lockdown hadn't really transformed my life at all as it has with others, it just opened my eyes on how delicate the world is and also, how hastily things can change.

To tell you the truth, it came down to watching our nation be told that we couldn't leave, that we wouldn't do certain things. We were isolated; we were at risk if we did the things we thought were once trivial.

We were trying to fight this thing in the world and for some reason; I saw an opportunity to do something while we saw the world tussle with this pandemic.

I told you once before, we intuitively get provoked. Maybe because everyone was doing those run five, nominate five at the start of April, something I couldn't do because of my asthma. Truth be told, I just started running because everyone else was doing it. Go with the flow right. It became a thing, it became a fad if anything, like baking became and the quizzes. But like those things, it evaporated, people lost interest.

For me when I was running a hundred and ninety-six days straight on the treadmill, I did it because no one thought I could do it and part of it was the gratification of proving people wrong. The satisfaction is not telling people about it. I never told anyone about the one hundred and ninety-six-day run, it was just a thing I was doing, it was as routine as brushing my teeth every morning. When you wake up in the morning, before anyone else, and smash out a four mile run, which was what I was doing before I dislocated my arm in 2019, I felt incredible - not because of the run, but incredible because I knew I was one of the only ones who was up and doing something with this time. It's like working on Christmas Day - you're doing something that no one else is doing, and that feeling alone is somewhat nourishing.

When I saw these fraudulent five kilometres times back in April so people could feel better about themselves, I felt sorry for them. I felt the whole purpose of running had gone out the window. Only until we got into a lockdown did we start running together because we were provoked to. Running is a beautiful thing, and I forgot that a long time ago. Running this challenge has inspired me to inspire others to find the love in running, to show people, that no matter what you have going on in your life, no matter what is happening in the world, you can make time to do this and that's what I wanted to inspire to others by doing the challenge and inspiring others to look at their time again and see what they could do it with it.

As routine goes, you start to distinguish every little thing like clockwork that is if you don't get obstacles like the weather or faulty headphones disrupting it. I had my alarm set half an hour later today knowing I would only have to run 4.4 miles. I could probably do that run in thirty minutes if I really went for it. The perspective I've got from this is: never brush anything away. At the start, I would say I couldn't do it because my legs had just run fifty odd days, twenty-nine of them running seven miles - but now I'm willing to believe I can do anything, and if I fail, then I go again. I genuinely didn't think I could run one of my later runs in less than an hour, but I did. Remember: the mindset is everything.

The sub thirty minute would be for another day though because Fran was going to be running with me today. I did my customary routine that I had kept up for the last month. My press ups, my toilet break, checking the weather.

Fran was enthused for me and was getting ready and sharing these moments with me. Something selfish came over me though. That this was my thing and these little build-ups to the actual runs were mine; I felt defensive about it. So, I kept to myself even though Fran was there. I didn't say a word to her. It didn't hit me until the last day, but these things were my mind preparing itself to do the run. Avoiding human contact was the key.

My body was fine and I was feeling great. Even more so, I was already thinking about what I want to do for July. I mean I had gotten so use to this routine - I wanted to keep a part of it. In the back of my mind, I just wanted to keep running. The time though recording it, editing the videos, talking about it, sharing it, just takes it away from you.

Sometimes you just need the road and your running trainers and that's it. That is what running is about. A part of me forgot that until today. With Fran so kindly doing the run with me on the last day, I comprehended so many things about why I run. Yes, last month I spent an hour alone just running and didn't really appreciate it at first, but the time you spend without anyone when running is a discovery about yourself, and it's always a new one with each run. Today was very scripted. It was a short run with someone taking photos of me and it was the last day. I didn't like anything about it, and it trumped the fact I was about to complete the two-hundred miles.

A destructive mind set can put any number of miles into a spin. As predicted, when we started running, and running at Fran's pace, I really was not relishing it. I fought that negativity. I decided to just enjoy it once again. The truth was, I was sad that it was coming to an end - but of course it was not. The challenge was coming to an end, but not my discovery for running. I still had a lot to learn about endurance, momentum, speed, timing, wind speed, strides, breathing, and general fatigue. I decided I wanted to learn everything there was to know about running, and it came to me on my very slow lap around Palmers Park.

Doing 4.4 miles meant two and half laps of the park before returning to home.

Fran was slower than usually, so slow that I think a fast-walking pace would have kept up with her, but she was really resolute. She pushed herself, but she ultimately came to a stop at the end of the first lap. She had never done that before, so I was a little concerned. She was okay though, as I was just jogging on the spot until I handed her my keys and then left her. I couldn't stop otherwise I knew I would have to start again. The whole two-hundred and ninety six miles I hadn't stopped; I couldn't stop now. She was okay - it had just been a while for her. The real reason is the mind set: she was so thrilled for me finishing the challenge, she forgot to get into that mind set before running. She didn't have a routine like I did to mentally prepare herself for the run. I think that's why she stopped.

We quickly exchanged words that she would take a photo of me when I finished, and then I ran off. In my head I just had to do one lap and then return home. I couldn't be sure where Fran would be to take the photo, but I shouldn't focus on that right now. Let's just get this run done.

The mentality of stopping really hit me when I was going back to my pace and realising, I only had one more lap left; and that's when it started to hurt.

Mile twelve is always one of the hardest when you do a half marathon, and that's basically where I was now. I managed to get back into my mind set; this was the last one ever and I was going to be done with it.

Last time I would see this tree or the Gurkhas for this challenge. My body was feeling great, in terms of no niggles or pains, just the mind telling me to stop. You just have to tell your mind to shut up and keep pushing your body. Watching SAS really helped me with keeping my head clear and learning how to fight the negativity. I learnt that if my body can do it, then I have no reason to stop. Unless my body fails me then I have to keep going otherwise I'm stopping because my head is saying to stop not my body and that for me, is failing.

Yes, okay, I've done the run but if I want to reach boundaries, if I want to discover how far I can go, what limits I can breach and set, then I need to trust my body to carry me and not let my mind dictate my decisions.

I reached the last lap and I saw Fran at the swings at the edge of the park. I'm glad she was okay, but I couldn't focus on her. As much as I wanted to pose, which I think I did anyways by sprinting past her, I could not draw my attention to her. I pretended not to look and whizzed past her, knowing she may get a few snaps, and kept my focus on the home stretch back.

I went past our local pub, which sits opposite Cemetery Junction, and I looked at my relive app for the first time; it was reading 4.4 miles. I began laughing and I just stopped running. It was only another 0.1 miles left to reach to my flat, but I stopped flat on my feet and just smiled.

I did it; I ran two-hundred miles in thirty days. I did it. It was Christmas morning to me. The day was finally here.

I started walking towards my flat when Fran rang, asking where I was. She was already at the entrance of the road where our flat is, ready to take the photo so she told me to just run back - and so I did. I saw her and just ran until she said stop. We smiled, we took photos, and we hugged. She gave me some moving and deep words about this challenge and all I had in my mind was: could I do this again?

My official mileage for June was 200.1 miles. It must have rounded up some of the miles but hey, can't always trust round numbers, can you? Remember: not everything is round numbers or conveniently perfect. The one hundred-metre record is not ten seconds, it's 9.58. The world doesn't take twenty-four hours to spin on its own axis, it takes twenty-three hours, fifty-five minutes and three seconds. We just round up.

Within minutes I had another fifty-pound donation and loads of messages congratulating me.

What I wanted now, was more. Routine shapes you; routine gives you a purpose for the day, but you can't let it control you. I now was ready for the next challenge. I felt powerful because I helped contribute towards a playground being built in eastern Africa and that brought so much delight to me. I chose to do that; I made that decision to run, all on my own. I had finished my two-hundred miles in June, but this was not the end.

The thing to take away from all of this is: I'm an average built guy with a hungry drive, and that is all it took. Yeah, I'm over six ft, yeah, I've got long legs - but when I had asthma early in the year and was putting on weight because of lockdown, I was becoming average, and to me, that's one of the worst things. Because I believe that everyone has a capability in them to push themselves in any aspect of their lives. Some people put these energies in the wrong things but there is energy there. It's about channelling that energy into something virtuous and when it comes to running or the start of something big, day one is always going to be the hardest and day two will maybe be hard too; but one thing you can take away from this, is that if you start something, you've made a massive step already. They next big step is seeing it through to its conclusion. Life is one big mystery; life doesn't always present you with clues or signs, and sometimes you need to force things to happen. We are only here for moments. Your life will come to an end, the ride will be over - but how much you enjoy the ride, how much you do on that ride, is entirely up to you. Don't spend the majority of your life queuing up for the ride. Get on it, enjoy it and go again. I provoke you to try.

1) The end of a challenge is a new beginning for the way you choose to see the world now. It should open doors, it should present paths and you might be ready to walk them, just like I did on day one and just like I have now on day thirty. Have a goal and take that first step.

2) What is it to be average, what is it to be like everyone else. Some, if not most, love going with the flow, sharing experiences with everyone, there is a comfort in that. There is nothing wrong with that but how much potential are you denying yourself, what achievements could you reach if you really wanted to. The scary thing is, it's actually possible to achieve it but it's about accepting the fact that you have to remove yourself from this norm, from this idea of what society dictates. You don't have to follow the norm to get there, if anything, the greater the goal, the more irregular the journey becomes and it's all part of it. Embracing it. Strive to be better, because you can.

3) The biggest step you can ever do is stepping out of your comfort zone and trying to do something out of the norm, something possibly out of your capability. The bigger the build-up, the longer it seems to reach. From day one, I couldn't even fathom reaching the 30th but day-by-day, you have to go through what life throws at you. Obstacles, maybe luck, maybe you just wake up on the wrong side of the bed, but you survive each day, and you move on to the next, developing every single day. Christmas always seems far away because of the build-up, but when you get there, it's glorious, it's magical because you've gone through that build up, the stress of buying presents, organising to see families, booking flights, arranging secret Santa but you know, it will come. The biggest lesson is just keep moving forward and you will be fine.

Epilogue

The challenges in our lives are everything. They will bring you to your knees; it may happen, but you have to get back up and fight, and get on with your day, despite how much the world is changing around you. Things won't go to plan, things haven't gone to plan - weddings have been cancelled, your job might be at risk, you might not be able to see your loved ones, but the most important thing is accepting these drastic changes and just doing what you can to get to this light at the end of a tunnel.

In time, stories will be told about this pandemic. Stories about what you did, what you had to do to adapt, to change your lifestyle. The lockdown introduced a new type of perspective for me; I don't know how it managed to achieve that, but it did. The why is not important - it's what I am going to do with this new way of seeing the world.

If I really wanted to stretch into why, I could. Maybe because I understand how fragile this world is, how fragile people can be, how much we rely on interaction, on these trivial things that suddenly get revoked. Maybe I wanted to inspire those people to think differently, to adapt differently.

The truth about this pandemic is it was unprecedented; it was completely new to our way of life, the repercussions of it. I don't think I was the only one to be rewarded with a new appreciate of life.

When it comes to running, it's all about the mind set on why you choose to run. Running is an escape; it's liberation from your world. It's a way of expressing yourself physically, running after an argument, running to rid a hangover, to simply get fit or just simply to burn off energy. It's awful for some, but magical for others. How can the same thing be both magical and awful?

Discovering who you are, what you're capable of starts with your appreciation on why you are here and what your purpose is. With that, takes times. Time to discover what your goal is and how you're going to get there. Time doesn't change, but what you do with your time can change.

For me, running was discovering myself, learning what I could do. Running is also a great metaphor for life, one stride at a time. The journey itself is hard but the end result is always rewarding. I gave myself a goal of fifty medals before I'm fifty. I don't know why but it gave my life purpose and with each challenge, with each run to achieving one more medal, I learn something new about myself every time. So, what did I learn whilst running 200.1 miles in June during lockdown? Do you really want to know?

Why don't you do it and find out for yourself. Because I can only speak for myself, I can only tell you about my journey whilst doing it. What will yours be, what obstacles will you face if you do it, what will happen to you when you complete it. What will happen if you fail, because that is okay, but you took that leap and if you take any leap into the unknown, it means you're curious about finding out more about yourself. I implore you to at least try, because you just never know what is waiting for you if you go for it.

Running Log

Date	Distance	Time	Distance 2	Time 2	Total Miles
June 1st	7 miles	1:03:49			7
June 2nd	7 miles	1:07:10			14
June 3rd	7 miles	1:01:44			21
June 4th	4.4 miles	41:10	3.4 miles	30:01	28.8
June 5th	7 miles	1:06:35			35.8
June 6th	7.5 miles	1:06:49			43.3
June 7th	3.6 miles (F)	38:40	4.4 miles	39:21	51.3
June 8th	7.5 miles	1:09:30			58.8
June 9th	3.8 miles	37:18	3.3 miles	29:02	65.9
June 10th	4.1 miles	38:55	2.9 miles	26:32	72.9
June 11th	4.1 miles (F)	46:05	3.7 miles	33:11	80.7
June 12th	4.1 miles	41:37	3.4 miles	31:26	88.2
June 13th	7.5 miles	1:08:34			95.7
June 14th	7 miles	1:08:35			102.7
June 15th	DAY OFF				102.7
June 16th	DAY OFF				102.7
June 17th	8 miles	1:15:39			110.7
June 18th	7.1 miles	1:08:04			117.8
June 19th	7 miles	1:07:58			124.8
June 20th	7.1 miles	1:07:49			131.9
June 21st	7 miles	1:05:08			138.9
June 22nd	7.8 miles	1:09:07			146.7
June 23rd	3.7 miles	35:44	3.4 miles	29:14	153.8
June 24th	6.8 miles	1:05:50			160.5
June 25th	7 miles	1:07:21			167.5
June 26th	7.1 miles	1:05:42			174.6
June 27th	7 miles	58:43			181.6
June 28th	7 miles	1:02:59			188.6
June 29th	7.1 miles	1:05:19			195.7
June 30th	4.4 miles	42:19			200.1

Running Data

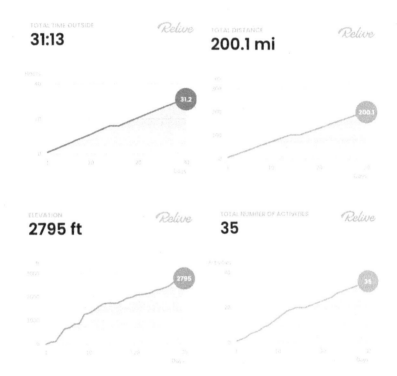

Acknowledgements

I will always be grateful for my friends and family who helped me get through this. Your simple kind words are enough to get me going. Your advice is always noted, sometimes acted on if I'm not being stubborn.

I cannot express enough thanks to my publishing team for their continual support and encouragement. James Essinger, there was never a dull conversation with yourself, and I thank you for all your help and guidance during the publishing stage. Charlotte Mouncey, you truly captured my vision to a tee. Thank you for your flexibility and productivity during the final stages.

A special mention to my cousin, Charlotte Painter, who is always on the other end of an email if I have a query. I thank you for your time and kindness.

Finally, my loving girlfriend Francesca. You saw this whole thing materialise to what it is, you were there from the beginning during those gruesome thirty days, the editing stages, the writing stages, every single comment I made towards it. Thank you for being you. Everything is always easier with you by my side. I love you and keep pushing me to be better.